Number Fifty-one in the Series of Keepsakes Issued for Its Members by the Friends of The Bancroft Library

PAST Tents

The Way We Camped

Susan Snyder

THE BANCROFT LIBRARY, UNIVERSITY OF CALIFORNIA, BERKELEY

HEYDAY BOOKS, BERKELEY, CALIFORNIA

Library of Congress Cataloging-in-Publication Data
Snyder, Susan, 1948-
Past tents : the way we camped / Susan Snyder.
p. cm.
ISBN 1-59714-039-2 (pbk. : alk. paper)
ISBN 1-59714-038-4 (hardcover : alk. paper)
1. Camping. 2. Tents. 3. Camping—Equipment and supplies.
I. Title
GV191.7.S68 2006
796.5409—dc22   2006013391

Cover Art: John and Annie Bidwell with their tent, 1898, Bancroft Portrait collection
Page i: "At lunch, Hazel Green," June 1888; John F. Young, Views in Yosemite Valley.
Pages ii–iii: "Overflow crowd of campers in Stoneman Meadow," circa 1915, from "Environmental Effects of Tourism at Yosemite National Park," manuscript.
Pages iv–v: "Going to make camp in a little meadow," Elizabeth Keith Pond, Yosemite, February 28, 1912; from the Marion Randall Parsons Papers.
Page 1: Muir Club, Girls' Outing, San Joaquin River and Evolution Basin, 1924, from the Leonarde Keeler Photograph Collection.

Cover Design: David Bullen Design
Interior Design / Typesetting: David Bullen Design
Printed in Canada by Friesens

Printed by Heyday Books in conjunction with The Bancroft Library, University of California, Berkeley. Orders, inquiries, and correspondence should be addressed to:
Heyday Books
P. O. Box 9145, Berkeley, CA 94709
(510) 549-3564, Fax (510) 549-1889
vwww.heydaybooks.com

10 9 8 7 6 5 4 3 2 1

Contents

Acknowledgments   vi

Introduction   vii

Hitting the Trail   2

Campsite Portraits   30

Pastimes   66

Hash and Ashcakes   90

Snags and Hitches   116

Campmates   128

Acknowledgments

The photographs and written selections in this book derive from many different sources in The Bancroft Library. There are the well-known, heavily used, multi-container collections such as the Sierra Club Papers, the papers of the LeConte and Keith-McHenry-Pond families, and the photographs of Frank Rodolph. But there are also the wonderfully exuberant, lovingly compiled, yet often unidentified albums of family vacations, loose undated snapshots, oral histories, and the diaries of ordinary folk—which all together fill in the pieces of a portrait of early rec-reational camping, its misfortunes and joys, trials and great fun. The library also houses papers of the various nineteenth-century geological surveys, the printed works of lettered journalists and writers of the outdoors, and the work of renowned artists such as Carleton Watkins, Ead-weard Muybridge, Charles Weed, Ansel Adams, Albert Bierstadt, and Thomas Ayers, who documented the taming and the framing of western wilderness for the growing populations of incipient camp-ers. These printed, manuscript, and visual materials that now reside on library shelves set the stage for the camping-for-fun phenomenon; they were the calls that beckoned people into the hills to experi-ence the geography and stay awhile.

Earnest thanks to the following people who made contributions to the mix: Ellen Byrne, Robert Chandler, James Eason, Jeannine Gendar, Tanya Hollis, Alice Q. Howard, Carole Howard, Jennifer Hu, Dan Johnston, Jessica Lemieux, Kathryn Kowalewski, Malcolm Margolin, Beth McGonagle, Erica Nordmeier, Kate Pope, Gene Rose, Mary Scott, Marc Selvaggio, Jim Snyder, Elizabeth Stephens, Lynette Stoudt, and my own campmate, Richard Neidhardt.

Introduction

Shortly after the California gold rush, a fundamental change occurred in the pitching of tents. Sleeping under the stars and cooking over an open fire had been matters of necessity and expediency in trackless wastes that concealed wild beasts and nightmare sounds. Wilderness had been the formless enemy to be conquered and crossed at all costs. But now the dark impenetrable woods and the fearsome wilds of folk legend gave way to the pressures of population, lumbering, mining, and agriculture. Now the trailblazers became pleasure trekkers, and trails that had been the routes of arduous travail became the paths of holiday jaunts. The dread and mystery lived on only in campfire tales and in the eerie shadows at the edge of the clearing shaped by the flames in the fire ring.

When the American frontier came to its conclusion on the shores of the Pacific, civilization had arrived in the West, and citizens were already seeking a respite from it. Rugged western landscapes were now admired for their sublime beauty, and the people who had crossed the formidable mountain ranges under duress and necessity now sought them out for adventure, relaxation, recuperation, and spiritual regeneration. The wilderness was under new management. The expanding populace took to the trails, to the railways, and then to the roads to get into what Thoreau in 1849 called a sanctuary from "the turmoil, the anxieties, and the hollowness of society," and from "the busy haunts of sordid money-making business." In 1878, essayist Charles Dudley Warner wrote in *Atlantic Monthly* that "the real enjoyment of camping and tramping in the woods lies in a return to primitive conditions of lodging, dress, and food, in as total an escape as may be from the requirements of civilization. It is wonderful to see how easily the restraints of society fall off." And so they did.

Camping was also championed for its curative powers. Removing oneself from the pestilential environment of the cities made for good digestion and good red blood. After the Reverend William H. H. Murray, on the East Coast in 1869, and Charles Nordhoff, in California in 1872, espoused the therapeutic value of the woods on both mind and body, people flocked to the hills seeking relief from their assorted ills. They believed that in particular "the dire parent of ills, dyspepsia," and consumption were helped by the curative powers of sleeping out of doors and breathing night breezes perfumed by spruce and pine. Mountain air was credited with causing "delicate ladies and fragile school-girls, to whom all food at home was distasteful and eating a pure matter of duty, to average a gain of a pound per day for the round trip." Nordhoff avowed that in April and May "there are canyons back of San Diego among the mountains, forty miles in the interior, where consumptives rapidly improved and recovered who experienced little benefit in the town itself."

It was early recognized that wilderness was finite, and that not everything on Earth had a purely utilitarian purpose. The nascent murmurings of the environmental movement followed closely on the heels of the outdoor movement. The natural world is, after all, the best place to learn that humans are ecologically and ethically involved in the larger community of life. The growing mobility of ordinary people and their increasing access to the natural landscape created a perfect opportunity for education. In 1891, Carter Harrison expressed frustration at the anthropocentric sentiment a woman in Yellowstone uttered while viewing the geysers: "One good housewife whom I met frequently at the different halting-places sighed deeply at the enormous waste of hot water, declaring there was enough here to laundry all America."

As more people visited the wild places

for recreation, the politics of preservation were also launched. William Colby of the Sierra Club said that John Muir's "idea was to educate as many people as possible about the value of the out-of-doors and wilderness. If people didn't know what was there, you couldn't get them to fight for it. But if they knew what was there, then they would fight to preserve it. This was one of the main reasons we started the outings in 1901."

With the transportation revolution came enhanced mobility. Modern gear meant a hefty increase in the use of parks and recreational lands, and camping grew in popularity. It was a relatively easy thing to pile the family, cots, and quilts into the car for a cheap vacation in the hills, picking up eggs and produce in the valley on the way. Though leisure had been reserved for the financially solvent, camping became the great economic leveler.

As use increased, the government's oversight of public lands grew, too. Veteran California forester Stuart Bevier

Show said in a 1965 oral history interview, "The Forest Service field forces changed quite rapidly in various ways, from an essentially negative attitude to forest recreation to a more positive one. Well, the totality of use continued to grow a great deal in the twenties, with roads and cars and more leisure time. You know, then as now, people would fight, bleed, and die for wilderness areas although they never go to that kind of country and never expect to go. They just like to know that they're around."

Once car camping became old hat, Airstreams and Winnebagos weren't far behind. John Steinbeck cast his vote for the luxuries of the travel trailer when he wrote in 1967, "Anyone who doesn't prefer a good bed in a warm room to lumpy pine boughs and a sleeping bag that feels like a plaster cast is either insane or an abysmal liar." But despite the proliferation of modern gear, there are still those who prefer the camp style of the early trampers. Going camping one hundred and fifty years ago was an exercise in independence, simplicity, conviviality. It offered a change of pace, splendor of scenery, and an opportunity to be close to nature and escape the trappings of society for a time. Despite the toil and hardship, and without the advantages of modern gear and freeze-dried food, people still eagerly packed up their duffle bags and took to the hills.

Every man is free
to loaf, and to
invite his soul.

"Nessmuk," 1884

"Companies A, B, and C of the Canyoneers," from Sierra Club Outing, July 1909, volume 2 (Tuolumne Meadows, Tuolumne Canyon and Hetch Hetchy) by E. T. Parsons and M. R. Parsons

A mountaineering couple, Edward and Marion Randall Parsons worked toward the establishment of the National Park Service. Marion edited John Muir's *Travels in Alaska* after his death.

{ O N E }

Hitting the Trail

When pleasure parties first took to the hills, they weren't particular about where they pitched their tents—alongside a railroad track, in a convenient farmyard or neighborly orchard—but they did do some sort of traveling before it was time to set up camp for the evening. Toting their duffles of assorted camping gear that Theodore Winthrop in 1863 called "multifarious wherewithals," they hit the trail on foot, on horseback, by steamboat, or on one kind of vehicle or another. Some depended on the local amenities, flora, and fauna to supply their vacation needs, and others took the servants, the kitchen sink, the living room rug, and the bathroom cabinet, lugging it all along with the help of wagons or mules, singing and sightseeing as they went.

"A Tramp up Mt. Tamalpais," circa 1880, from the Frank B. Rodolph Photograph Collection

Frank Rodolph, pictured on the trail, second from left, toting his photographic equipment, was a commercial photographer active in Oakland during the 1870s and 1880s. An inveterate camper and diarist, he was an ardent member of an adventuring club, the Merry Tramps of Oakland. A group of nature-loving friends, the Merry Tramps ranged around California on annual excursions until 1890, taking trains, ferries, wagons, and horses to reach their destinations.

An excellent Norwegian recipe for waterproofing leather is this: Boil together two parts pine tar and three parts cod-liver oil. Soak the leather in the hot mixture, rubbing in while hot. It will make boots waterproof, and will keep them soft for months, in spite of repeated wettings.

Horace Kephart, *The Book of Camping and Woodcraft* (New York: Outing Publishing Co., 1906)

Librarian Kephart left St. Louis to become a passionate outdoorsman, campaigning vigorously for the creation of the Great Smoky Mountains National Park in North Carolina and Tennessee.

Bohemian Grove hiker Joseph Mailliard, Sonoma County, California, July 1921; Charles Fremont Pond, photographer; from the Keith-McHenry-Pond Family Papers

Ornithologist, wit, and raconteur Joseph Mailliard camped throughout the coastal West collecting for the California Academy of Sciences. His pursuit of bird specimens began, when he was fifteen, with a Townsend's solitaire egg carried down Yosemite's Glacier Point trail in a handkerchief.

"Dorothy and Ned Atkinson brought down from Glacier Point via the Four Mile Trail on the burro Plum Duff, circa 1886," from the Francis P. Farquhar Pictorial Collection

An early conservationist and the director of the Sierra Club for twenty-seven years, Francis Farquhar wrote *Place Names of the High Sierra* in 1926 and *History of the Sierra Nevada* in 1965. He climbed every 14,000-foot mountain on the West Coast and, with his wife, Marjory Bridge Farquhar, was a pioneer of Sierra Nevada climbing for forty years.

"Lucy and the pack dogs on
the way to the Wild Man's,"
undated, from the Sierra
Club Portrait Collection

STANDARD ALPINE RUCK SACK

The favorite pack of the Swiss mountaineers, as it conforms to the shape of the body and sets close, so that it will not over-balance. It is intended for average packs, and is made of double texture, olive-colored canvas, thoroughly waterproof, the sack being 18x18 inches with two outside pockets in addition, with buckle flaps for small articles. The opening at the top is closed with a draw string with a protecting flap buckling down over it when in use. Shoulder straps of strong webbing and leather are adjustable and are ribbed from the center of the top to each of the lower corners of the sack. The outside pockets and the opening of the sack are reinforced by leather binding. All buckles are leather bound.

Our No. H 401—Weight, 1½ lbs. Each. Postpaid......$3.50

HIKER'S TAMALPAIS LIGHT PACK SACK

Was designed by a prominent sportswoman for general use. It has boxed sides and bottom with rounded corners, making it more roomy than other bags of the same size, with a detachable pocket inside the bag for small articles, and a large pocket for change of shoes. There are two partitions for toilet articles on the under side of a flap that extends over the bag and buckles down to its bottom. Coat or sweater can be carried between the flap and the bag proper. Buckle leather shoulder straps are rigged from the corners of the bag, which is tape bound and strongly reinforced at every wearing point. Made of Antiwet duck, also of standard olive khaki. Postpaid.

Our No. H 410—Antiwet duck; 16 oz. Each...........$3.25

THE "GO LIGHT" RUCK SACK

Modeled after the Alpine sack and is an ideal pack when "going light." It is oblong in shape, closes with draw string, also has turn-down flap over top of sack and is provided with one large inside pocket. It is rigged the same as No. H 293, the adjustable shoulder straps being of leather. We make this bag of our Antiwet duck and of Government standard olive khaki, either of which when empty, can be carried in the pocket. Size, 15x19 inches.

Our No. H 406—Antiwet duck; wt. 12 oz. Postpaid.$2.50
Our No. H 407—Standard khaki; wt. 9 oz. Postpaid 2.00

DOUBLE-END DUNNAGE BAG

Our standard, made of 8-oz. double filled Pacific duck. Is used extensively for camping; can be carried or slung across either riding or pack saddle. Size 4 ft. x 12 in.

Our No. H 416—Each. Postpaid...........$2.50

HEAVY LOAD PACK HARNESS

A harness that is adaptable to all sizes and shapes of packs. It has a deep and wide shoulder yoke of heavy canvas, strongly reinforced, the extra wide shoulder and breast straps also the buckle straps that holds the pack, all being of a high grade oak tanned leather.

NOTE—We also make this harness with an adjustable leather head strap the use of which distributes the weight over shoulders, neck and head. Illustration shows the harness attached to a duffle bag to better illustrate its shape.

Our No. H 425—Harness alone. 1¼ lbs. Postpaid..$4.80
Our No. H 426—With head strap. 1¾ lbs. Postpaid 5.85

SIERRA CLUB PACK STRAPS

This strap harness is a modification of the original and heavy Alaska pack harness. It is made of strong but light bridle leather, firmly riveted at all points of strain. It consists of regular knapsack shoulder straps, adjustable to any size, and has two straps to circle the pack sidewise, also one that passes over the pack lengthwise. Weight, 19 ounces.

Our No. H 430—Each, complete. Postpaid............$2.75

KIT CARRYING STRAPS

A practical harness that is light, and easily adjustable to fit both individual and size of pack. Will render uncommon service, being made from haversack and rifle straps of highest grade leather of U. S. Army stipulation. The carrying straps are wider over the shoulders, easing pressure at that point. Length of straps, 50 in.

Our No. H 433—Each. Postpaid..$2.00

WEB TRUNK AND PARCEL STRAPS

Straps that are ideal for trunk or any parcel or package. Specially made and very flexible, being superior to leather for strength and wear. Have lock-fast or non-slip buckles. (Postpaid.)

Our No. H 446—Each. 10 ft. by 1¼ in. wide............$1.00
Our No. H 447—Each. 8 ft. by 1¼ in. wide........ 0.75
Our No. H 448—Each. 6 ft. by 1¼ in. wide........ 0.50

Special Outing Goods Catalog,
the Ellery Arms Company,
San Francisco, California, 1922

A shoulder pack can be improvised as follows: Take a grain sack and place a pebble an inch or more in diameter in each of the lower corners. Tie one leg of a pair of overalls to each of these corners. (The pebble prevents the knot from slipping off.) To close the sack tie the mouth of it and the waist of the overalls tightly with a cord. The legs make comfortable shoulder straps.

Handbook for Campers in the National Forests in California, U.S. Department of Agriculture, Forest Service (Washington, D. C.: Government Printing Office, 1915)

Starting out for a day's tramp in the woods, he would ask whether we wanted to take a "reg'lar walk, or a random scoot" — the latter being a plunge into the pathless forest. And when the way became altogether inscrutable — "Waal, this is a reg'lar random scoot of a rigmarole."

Charles Dudley Warner celebrating an Adirondack guide of his acquaintance named Phelps in "In the Wilderness," *Atlantic Monthly,* June 1878

Portrait of Norman Clyde, North Fork of Lone Pine Creek, August 17, 1931, from the Francis P. Farquhar Photograph Collection

Norman Clyde, known as "the pack that walked like a man," traveled from one of his hundreds of outdoor "living rooms" or "hotels" to the next. These isolated campsites were scattered in every corner of the Sierra and were selected for their firewood and water supplies and scenic inspiration. A mountaineer legendary for over one hundred first ascents in California, Clyde was also a teacher and guide, leading camping parties well into his seventies.

We camped on a little snow-free patch of rock on the frozen lake in the Palisades that early-season trip long ago. I can still remember my awe at the collection of gear Norman drew out of his duffle bag. There's part of the weight right there. The duffle bag was lashed to a six-pound Yukon pack frame which also supported a full length Hudson Bay axe. But perhaps the kitchen bag was the most surprising to Hubert and me, as our meager assortment of pans scrounged from depression cupboards was no match for Norman's six large kettles, the cups and spoons, the dishes and bowls, the salt shakers, condiments, servers and graters and, for all I know, cookie cutters. I can remember my astonishment at seeing his special stick-mop for washing dishes. And he even had extra food for us! . . . Perhaps the duplications in Norman's list contrasted most strongly with our Boy Scout style. Boots? He carried several; ski boots, tricouni boots, rubber-soled boots for the rocks, camp slippers. "It's not true that I carry an anvil in my pack. Only this little piece of iron to put in the heel for replacing tricounis. That's something these go-lightly boys never think about. Some gaffer is always tearing out some nails and needing repairs. And anyway, if I want to carry a rock in my pack to keep me steady down the trail, that's my business." A camera? Norman carried five. That's right. A 35mm loaded with Ansco and one with Eastman film, a 120 for black and white and another 120 for color, and of course his "throw-in-the-lake" camera, which was the spare. A book for evening reading? Well, Norman usually travels alone and on long trips, so he had a rather large library in many languages. "They last longer, especially the Greek as I'm usually a little rusty in that.". . .We weighed one of those loads once . . . the pack weighed out at ninety-two pounds.

Smoke Blanchard, remembering Norman Clyde in a letter to Dave Bohn, in *Norman Clyde of the Sierra Nevada,* edited by Dave Bohn (Berkeley, Calif.: Scrimshaw Press, 1971)

A wiry man, of slight build, all muscle and sinew, he was able to traverse great distances on foot, climb precipices and the walls of glaciers with steady nerves, subsist on the smallest possible allowances of food, and sleep where night found him, with no covering but the light clothing which he had worn during the heat of the day. His needs were of the smallest — a bag of bread, a little sack of tea, and a cup in which to steep it — that was the only outfit he carried, beyond his notebook and his four scientific instruments — a thermometer, a barometer, a clinometer, and a watch. Sometimes, when he had nearly reached the top of a mountain and expected to return the same way, he would leave his bag of food and trust to finding it on his return. No matter how wild and rough the country, nor how far he had gone, nor how stormy the weather, he never lost his way, nor failed to find the particular gorge among a thousand where the bread-bag was hidden. Sometimes he missed three or four or even a greater number of meals without special inconvenience. And it was always something of a cross to him to be compelled, when the bag was empty, to return from his heights to what he called the "bread line."

Ray Stannard Baker, "John Muir," in *The Outlook,* June 1903

John Muir with hikers, lower end of Tuolumne Meadows, July 18, 1909; Walter L. Huber, photographer; Bancroft Portrait Collection

John Muir, preeminent naturalist and conservationist, has been called the father of our national parks but once described himself as a "poetico-trampo-geologist-botanist-ornithologist-naturalist, etc." His writings contributed greatly to the creation of Yosemite, Sequoia, Mount Rainier, Petrified Forest, and Grand Canyon National Parks and inspired federal conservation programs. In 1892, he formed the Sierra Club "to make the mountains glad." He was the club's first president, an office he held until his death in 1914.

District engineer for the United States Forest Service, California and Nevada, Walter Huber was instrumental in blocking the flooding of Devils Postpile National Monument by a dam on the San Joaquin River, and later became president of the Sierra Club.

Bathe sore feet at night in warm water and apply Vaseline or tallow. If not well in the morning, coat the inside of the stockings, as well as the feet, with soap or tallow. A very sore spot should be covered with a piece of surgeon's plaster, which will effectually prevent chafing. Blisters should be threaded through and the thread cut off at each side of the blister, leaving a piece within to facilitate the escape of water; cover with a vaselined rag. On no account pull any skin off. Put raw pine pitch on corns.

Edward Breck, *The Way of the Woods* (New York: G. P. Putnam's Sons, 1908)

I saw three maidens 'neath a tree
And they were strange as strange could be,
Their hair hung down like the three weird sisters
As they sat on the ground and counted their blisters;
And a candle in a tomato can
Cast its flickering light around
As they sat and gibbered upon the ground,
As they sat and gibbered and counted their blisters
For the Colby mile makes all maids sisters.
It raises the blisters,
It raises the blisters.

Nelson Hackett, "The First Day's March,"
from the Irma Weill Papers, 1916

Chafed heels can be alleviated by rubbing soap into the socks.

Handbook for Campers in the National Forests in California, U.S. Department of Agriculture, Forest Service (Washington, D.C.: Government Printing Office, 1915)

"Oh, for some adhesive tape!" Sierra Club High Trip, Mt. Ritter, Yosemite National Park, July 22, 1914, from the Sierra Club Photograph Albums

Contrary to expectation, [the horse] Luckee trotted off at the tail of the wagon without remonstrance, until at Niles, a sharp western breeze met them, and Millie gave her big shawl a flirt, preparatory to settling it on her shoulders. He did not say much then; but the two horses in front suddenly came to a dead stop, to their own apparent astonishment, for they were evidently pulling as hard as ever; and a backward glance revealed Luckee sitting on his haunches, head thrown back, a certain expression of desperate resolution pervading his whole person, and the rawhide rope stretched to its utmost tension. Millie was obliged to freeze for five minutes, and then by cautious degrees to resume the alarming shawl. Halfway to Decoto the stick in the end of the grain sack hammock slipped and rattled against the wheel; down went Luckee on his haunches again. After he had snapped a brand new take rope like packthread, Jo got out and mounted him, leaving the lines in Millie's hands. Away went horse and rider, and alone along the road trotted the double team with the gypsyish load, and a small solitary figure in faded green suit, muffled awkwardly about the neck and shoulders with the big brown plaid shawl, and surmounted by a big Chinese straw hat with straight brim, sitting on the front seat, upon Jo's pistol as she afterward learned, holding the lines in hands hitherto held incapable of guiding a double team by tender parents and brothers.

Milicent Washburn Shinn, H.U.C. [Hard-Up-Crowd], manuscript, 1881

Milicent Shinn kept a collaborative journal of a two-week 1881 camping trip taken to the redwoods, "down toward Pescadero," by four men and four women, all UC Berkeley students, who called themselves the Hard-Up-Crowd, or H.U.C. Their gear included a thirty-five-pound box of cherries, a tent, hammocks, two pair of blankets apiece, a limited number of cooking utensils, and a somewhat less limited number of things to eat, all accommodated in the Shinn "Dimmyphrat" wagon, drawn by Mr. Davis' graceful horse "Bummer" plus a Shinn horse, Luckee, and Bob the dog. The H.U.C. was comprised of Selim M. Franklin, Rhoda Tucker, Joseph Clark Shinn, Jane Barry, Ellen Davis, Carroll Davis, Edward Clark Sanford, and Milicent Shinn. She became the editor of the Overland Monthly *at the age of twenty-five in 1882 and was the first woman to receive a doctorate from the University of California, in 1898.*

"Moving in Big Basin," Santa Cruz County,
California; A. Breuner, photographer; from
the Sierra Club Photograph Albums

"Going to make camp in a little meadow," Elizabeth Keith Pond, Yosemite, February 28, 1912; from the Marion Randall Parsons Papers

After Charles Fremont Pond retired from the Navy, he and his daughter Elizabeth Keith Pond took frequent long hikes and camping trips throughout California, which she described in her series of illustrated Mountain Journals.

YOLO BASE LINE.

THE MOVABLE TENT OR "YOLO BUGGY,"
51 feet long, under which all measurements were made.

"The movable tent or 'Yolo Buggy',"
from Photographs of the Yolo Base
Line, California, 1881; Werner
Suess, photographer

A photographer for the U.S.
Coast and Geodetic Survey and
an inventor, Werner Suess is also
credited with improvements to
the gramophone.

Outfit

Horse furniture

Saddle and bridle. Saddle blankets. Thongs in plenty. Lariat 25–30 feet. Hitch rope 10 ft.

Personal Furniture

Blankets. Change of flannel shirt. Change of underware. Overalls. Belt and knife. Pistol. Comb, brush, and tooth brush. Soap and towel. Handkerchiefs (red). Needles & thread. Buttons. Maps and note book. Postal cards. Matches.

Medicines

Whiskey in flask (N.B.). Ginger. Quinine pills. Laxative pills. Court plaster.

Pack

Pack saddle & bags. 2 frying pans. 1 bread pan 2 camp kettles. Tin plates, one for each and 2 or 3 additional. One tin cup for each. Spoons ditto. Knives and forks ditto. Big spoon. Tea pot (riveted) Bar soap. Dish towels. Bags a plenty Ball of twine

Provisions

Flour 50 lbs. Bacon (best). Royal baking powder. Sugar 15–20 lbs. Salt & pepper. Mush. Rice. Tea 3–5 lbs. Coffee 10 lbs. Lard in tight can. Butter in tight can. Axe. Oil cloth for table. Matches. Condensed milk Dried fruit? Potatoes, milk, eggs, meat to be bought on the way as desired.

LeConte Family Papers
Diary entry, Joseph Nisbet LeConte, camping trip to Hetch Hetchy and Yosemite, 1889

Teacher, geologist, and outdoorsman Joseph LeConte's youngest offspring, Joseph "Little Joe" Nisbet LeConte, an electrical engineer and an avid mountaineer, kept camping diaries from 1887 to 1946. This 1889 trip to Hetch Hetchy and Yosemite was made by father and son, along with three fellow University of California students: Ross Morgan, Charles Palache, and Charles Merrill. The four nineteen-year-olds together were known as the Jolly Jaunting Juniors. They traveled to a number of peaks in the Yosemite backcountry just a short time before it became a national park.

Muletrain on switchbacks,
Sierra Club outing, circa 1938;
Charles Webber, photographer;
from the Sierra Club Pictorial
Miscellany

I figured the 200 members of the party and the 50 packers, cooks, dishwashers, and helpers would eat 600 pounds of fairly concentrated food (dry cereals, dehydrated vegetables, etc.) a day at the start of a trip. By the end of the outing they'd be eating 800 pounds a day. One very interesting fact was the consumption

Sierra Club High Trip packer
Sam Marks (?), undated, from
the Sierra Club Portrait Collection

of sugar. I've forgotten how much sugar we took along but it was a tremendous amount. Let's see. It'd be a ton and a half.... A ton and a half for 250 people for a month.... The consumption of sugar would increase with colder weather.

William E. Colby, interviewed by Hal Roth, February 27, 1961, manuscript

Colby initiated and led the annual Sierra Club outings beginning in 1901 and continued to do so for thirty years. The outings, attended by up to two hundred people at a time, eventually became too large and detrimental to the landscape in the 1950s and were discontinued.

"Sharing breakfast with Banjo Eyes in camp by the Roaring River," June 22, 1926; Elizabeth Keith Pond Mountain Journals, Keith-McHenry-Pond Family Papers

Old Jiggs, our mule, was most lovable, but he was quite unaware that we were running the trip. He was thirsty in the middle of each ford, famished at the sight of every wisp of grass, and susceptible to wanderlust each time we rested; but these faults were as nothing. His racial idiosyncrasy of one single forward speed on ups, downs, and levels was, however, most exasperating. On an uphill stretch he was usually resting his head upon my packboard, pushing, and blowing sweet words in my ear. Then, as the trail dropped, my customary step-out would be suddenly curbed as I reached my rope's end, and there was definite indication that nothing I might do would change matters. By the time we reached Fifth Lake I was thoroughly subjugated to the desires of the dumb animal, and a much faster uphill climber than I had ever desired to be.

David Ross Brower, "Far from the Madding Mules," in the *Sierra Club Bulletin*, vol. 20, no. 1, February 1935

Over a lifetime of camping, climbing, and ski mountaineering, David Brower made seventy first ascents in the Western U.S. He was the executive director of the Sierra Club for seventeen years, founder of Earth Island Institute, the League of Conservation Voters, and Friends of the Earth, and became known as the Archdruid of the environmental movement for his dynamic activism.

The pails we had, instead of being circular in section, were rectangular, and for convenience in carrying were made so as to "nest." … We carried our pails in a wooden frame, strapped in front of the handle of one bicycle, and we put the soap and towels inside the smallest one. This arrangement rattled so much that the hitherto silent steed was dubbed by one of our party the "ice-wagon." Our principal reason for undertaking a camping trip on bicycles was to save expense. Upon our return we figured up that, exclusive of some repairs, but including expenses on the boat to Sacramento and railroad fare from Stockton to San Francisco, we had spent $12.85 each during the two weeks. But we found that this way of traveling is not only economical, but is also ideal for the mountain lover.

Roy R. Dempster, "Camping A-Wheel," in the *Sierra Club Bulletin*, vol. 2, no. 2, March 1897

"Joe Pierce and friends from college," June 3, 1889:
Joseph C. Pierce, Stanley C. Smith, and Edwin C.
Edwards, Bancroft Portrait Collection

A vacation spent in the saddle of a motor-
cycle is one of the least expensive. As far as
the actual cost of travel is concerned, it may
be reckoned at less than a cent a mile. When it
comes to food and lodging, one may live like
a pioneer or a prince. A knapsack, a rifle, and
a fishing rod will dissipate the specter of the
cost of living. One may sleep under the stars,
or, if one is very particular, under the kind
of a tent that soldiers carry when campaigning. The motorcyclist is able to get so far from
the beaten track that he will find himself, if he
chooses, for days at a time in places where they
tell the hours by the sun and have to look in the
almanac to fix the days of the week.

Thaddeus S. Dayton, "The Motor-Cyclist's Vacation,"
in *Harper's Weekly*, August 3, 1912

"D. A. Stivers and Thor arrive
in camp, Camp Kitmear, 1915,"
from Panama Pacific International
Exposition and Yosemite Camping
Views

"Our first camp at Yellow Stone Park. Note table—
The geyser at hand made laundry-work a snap—
just tie a string to a shirt and let her boil." From the
Leo W. Meyer, G. C. Degener, and A. T. Ehrenpfort
Photographs, Transcontinental Auto Tour, 1917

Our first camp at Yellow Stone Park. note table.— The geyser at hand mad
laundry-work a snap—just tie a string to a shirt and let her boil.

They would have to get up real early and carry all the mattresses, blankets, cooking equipment, and food down the long flights of stairs to the auto. I can't figure out how they got it all squeezed in. The only place for carrying our luggage was a very small space in back of the front fenders and behind the spare tire that was by the side of the car or on the running board. There was no trunk or carrying space at the back of the car. If anything was carried inside it would have to be in front of the passengers' legs and they would be very cramped. The back seat was only wide enough to hold three passengers and there was only room for two in the front. As there were five grown-ups I guess I had to sit on someone's lap. My grandfather, grandmother, my aunt, mother, father, and I were all squeezed in. . . . My grandmother had baked a pillowslip full of cookies for the trip.

In 1921 with our new Seven Passenger Chandler we went camping to Yosemite. My father bought a large tent that was twelve by fourteen feet in size. He bought this tent from a man who worked for the City of San Francisco. It was one that was used by the people who lost their homes during the earthquake and fire of 1906. He also bought four folding steel beds and five folding chairs. The steel beds weighed sixty-five pounds each. He made a large folding table. The mattresses were just heavy cotton quilts that were made to protect the enamel stoves when they were delivered. They were new quilts that would later be used in his stove store. Each one of us had one blanket that did not keep out the cold. For cooking we had a fine three burner gasoline stove on a stand. Oil lanterns were used for light. Our clothing was stored in canvas bags that Uncle Charley Carlson made. They were like the ones the sailors used to store their things on the ship. A large box was made for one running board that held all the canned goods and the food.

[In 1924] my father made up a string of electric lights that could be plugged into the car battery for lighting up the tent and the kitchen table. I brought along a collection of flashlights including my prized three bulb flashlight that I won for getting subscriptions to the *San Francisco Examiner*. It had a white light in the center and a red and green light. It had three batteries and three switches.

Erwin Strohmaier, "California History: Early Vacations," Erwin Strohmaier Family Papers

Erwin Jack Strohmaier, in addition to helping his father, Jacob, in the family's stove and appliance store in Oakland, was a photographer for the Air Force in World War II.

"Mrs. Perrelet. The fliver. Miss Muth,"
Death Valley Automobile Trip, 1926

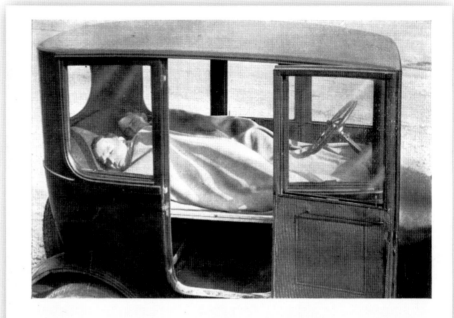

John D. Long and J. C. Long, *Motor Camping* (New York: Dodd, Mead, 1926)

Two views of the Foldaway bed for Ford sedans; above, showing it in use for the night, and below, serving as a part of a dressing room

Mary Roberts Coolidge, circa 1916; Dane Coolidge, photographer; from the Bancroft Portrait Collection

Sociologist Mary Coolidge wrote *The Rain-Makers: Indians of Arizona and New Mexico* in 1929, and coauthored *The Navajo Indians* with her husband, Dane Coolidge, in 1930.

TWO

Campsite Portraits

The location, character, and décor of campsites were as varied as their inhabitants. Because it took longer to reach their wilderness destinations, campers stayed out longer, and over time, their campsites evolved into individualized outdoor homes, with belongings hung handily on trees, rocks, and ropes, and on makeshift shelves. There were secret swimming holes and favored thicket dressing rooms, convenient log benches for al fresco dining, and just the right campfire ring and upwind tent placement. Camps ranged from the simplest blanket-and-fry-pan outfit to elaborate, open-air housekeeping extravaganzas. As they do today, campers transported their lifestyles and personalities to their campsites.

Annie Montague Alexander and Louise Kellogg in front of Egyptian tent, Last Chance Gulch, Kern County, California, September 1924; Mary Charlotte Alexander, photographer; courtesy of Alice Q. Howard

During a six-week field trip to collect specimens for Berkeley's Museum of Vertebrate Zoology, Annie Alexander, Louise Kellogg, and Mary Charlotte Alexander used an Arab tent they had purchased in Cairo and which in Egypt had required fourteen men to raise the fifteen-foot center pole. In their camp northwest of the Mojave Desert, the three women managed to erect it themselves. They furnished it with twelve brightly colored panels embroidered with Byzantine designs and Arabic good-luck phrases. Bedouin rugs covered the sand, making the tent a welcome respite from the midday desert sun.

We plodded on, two or three hours longer, and at last the Lake [Tahoe] burst upon us—a noble sheet of blue water lifted six thousand three hundred feet above the level of the sea, and walled in by a rim of snow-clad mountain peaks that towered aloft full three thousand feet higher still! It was a vast oval, and one would have to use up eighty or a hundred good miles in traveling around it. As it lay there with the shadows of the mountains brilliantly photographed upon its still surface I thought it must surely be the fairest picture the whole earth affords.

We found the small skiff belonging to the Brigade boys, and without loss of time set out across a deep bend of the lake toward the landmarks that signified the locality of the camp. I got Johnny to row—not because I mind exertion myself, but because it makes me sick to ride backwards when I am at work. But I steered. A three-mile pull brought us to the camp just as the night fell, and we stepped ashore very tired and wolfishly hungry. In a "cache" among the rocks we found the provisions and the cooking utensils, and then, all fatigued as I was, I sat down on a boulder and superintended while Johnny gathered wood and cooked supper. Many a man who had gone through what I had would have wanted to rest.

It was a delicious supper—hot bread, fried bacon, and black coffee. It was a delicious solitude we were in, too. Three miles away was a saw-mill and some workmen, but there were not fifteen other human beings throughout the wide circumference of the lake. As the darkness closed down and the stars came out and spangled the great mirror with jewels, we smoked meditatively in the solemn hush and forgot our troubles and our pains. In due time we spread our blankets in the warm sand between two large boulders and soon fell asleep, careless of the procession of ants that passed in through rents in our clothing and explored our persons. Nothing could disturb the sleep that fettered us, for it had been fairly earned, and if our consciences had any sins on them they had to adjourn court for that night, anyway. The wind rose just as we were losing consciousness, and we were lulled to sleep by the beating of the surf upon the shore.

It is always very cold on that lake shore in the night, but we had plenty of blankets and were warm enough. We never moved a muscle all night, but waked at early dawn in the original positions, and got up at once, thoroughly refreshed, free from soreness, and brim full of friskiness. There is no end of wholesome medicine in such an experience.

Mark Twain, *Roughing It* (Hartford, Conn.: American Pub. Co., 1872)

Mark Twain's second major work is about going west to mine for wealth in the earth of Nevada and finding it instead as a writer. The situations in Roughing It *were based on the real experiences of Samuel Clemens in his westering migration.*

"And then there is 'the stillness, the silence, with the peace of the world piled on top.'" Elizabeth Keith Pond Mountain Journals, January 17, 1914, during a trip from Yosemite Valley to Tuolumne Meadows; from the Keith-McHenry-Pond Family Papers.

Last night was what I call "roughing it." Towards evening it turned much warmer and the snow came down thick and fast. Then the wind arose in great gusts; sometimes moaning through the trees overhead and then afar off down the Valley. Flashes of lightning surrounded us and peals of thunder came echoing along the cliffs. After darkness was upon us, great masses of snow still dropped down from the surrounding trees and there was no rest, for one had to keep raising the canvas overhead to keep the weight from one's head. By midnight there was over a foot of fresh snow banked on either side of us and when I could no longer hear Charlie turning or breathing or the faintest rustle of his canvas, I could not help but think he had smothered, so I would then call frantically until I could hear a faint muffled voice from afar saying, "I'm all right, Bessie. How are you? Are your feet warm?

Keep your blankets pulled well over your head and the snow off as much as you can." Then just as I would be dozing off after having found a comfortable position, I would hear, "Bessie, oh, Bessie, are you all right?" And so the night wore on with the peculiar soft splashing sound of the large flakes alighting on your balloon silk and waiting and wondering if it would ever cease falling. Finally, in spite of all my strenuous elbow and knee work, I became so tightly wedged that I could scarcely turn over and the snow bank at my head had risen to about two feet, so that I could not get enough air. I managed with difficulty to draw up both knees and pulled up to a sitting position, with my blankets drawn tight around my chin to keep the wind out, and so I remained waiting for the dawn. At daylight two heads and two pairs of shoulders arose almost simultaneously above the snow line and eyes looked out upon a white world, earth and everything thereon and sky of the same grayish white hue. Our cozy little camp of two nights before had vanished; even the sled was buried and the white surface was calm and unruffled except where two

heads stuck out above the snow line. But a few minutes were used in discussing the situation. A lean-to we must have if we were to enjoy any comfort that day and night, so at half past seven we arose in the midst of the blizzard and set to work with a will to erect a shelter. First Charlie cut five small dead trees for the frame over which we stretched one of the pieces of balloon silk, securing it at each corner with thong. At the foot and side we placed boughs and then cut and dragged in enough boughs to line the whole and make a soft, sweet bed. While Charlie cut boughs and wood, I was busily engaged in digging out the food bags, frying pan, kettles, etc. The lean-to complete, blankets shaken out and transferred, wood cut, and fire laid took until noon and then we had a fine meal after a day of prunes and chocolate. We stood off and admired the beautiful little picture that we had created, and then crawled back as fast as we could into our blankets.

Elizabeth Keith Pond, "Mountain Journal II," Yosemite, January 1914, Keith-McHenry-Pond Family Papers

Well-tested hints:

1. The tail of your sweater is fine for darning if you unravel a bit of it.

2. If thirsty and without water, put a small stone or a button under your tongue; it will keep your mouth moist.

3. A well-soaked cloth wrapped around a bottle will keep it cool. Hang it up in a breeze in the shade.

4. A little vinegar in water boiled in your pots or pans will take away the smell of fish.

5. Remember it is warmer to sleep in a snowdrift than on the bare ground.

6. Talk to your dog or horse — he is just as lonely as you are.

7. If your boots are wet, scrape away some hot dirt or sand from under the fire and fill them with it. They will be dry in the morning.

8. To avoid sore feet, wear large shoes with small hob nails that cannot be felt through the soles, a thin pair of socks, soaped on the heels on the inside next to the feet, and a heavy pair of woolen socks over them. This will positively prevent blisters.

9. A reserve match supply can be kept dry, even if soaked in water, by emptying the box and pouring melted paraffin over layer after layer of matches.

Camp Craft and Woodlore, Canadian National Railways, undated

June and July were comparatively restful months to me, for I fled "far from the madding crowd" and from the numberless persons who, without even a pretence of acquaintance, pursued me at all hours and into all places, to extort from me time, money, influence, sympathy, and whatever else they fancied I had. I found that in order to save a modicum of strength for the necessary demands of an intricate business, and to assure a convalescence from a severe illness, I must hie to parts unknown to the mass, so I selected a hidden spot in the hills back of one of our vineyards in Sonoma County, and set up a camp home. I planned the details so as to secure all available comfort in such a life, and the two months' rest has amply repaid all outlay in that direction.

I had the tents made of good size, eighteen by sixteen feet, and fifteen feet height to the ridgepole, and board floors elevated enough to prevent the accumulation of dampness. A very opportune purchase of some Turkish rugs gave us the warmth and cheer that bare floors would have lacked and a home-like look and feeling were imparted by putting a little stove into the

Phoebe Apperson Hearst in tent, Sonoma County, California, circa 1891.
From the George and Phoebe Apperson Hearst Photograph Collection

Phoebe Apperson Hearst, University of California regent and benefactress, and matriarch of the Hearst newspaper family, took refuge in Sonoma County from the clamors of society at the suggestion of her husband, George.

sitting-room tent. Screens enabled us to partition off our tents for toilet purposes, and steady little oak tables held our toilet appliances.

I never saw the joke or enjoyment in talking about sleeping on the "soft side of a board," so did not try to solve that problem, but had comfortable spring beds and hair mattresses on each bedstead. Some of these bedsteads were pretty designs in iron and brass, the iron being enameled white with a delicate tracery of gilding on wider parts.

In my room, I had a capacious oak desk, and if I had taken no papers at all with me, that desk would have been only ample for the flood of mail that reached me. In our sitting-room, there were a willow table, lounge couch, abundance of rocking chairs, and down cushions, two screens with bamboo frames and covers of Morris prints, and a bronze lamp with an old-gold silk shade. The lamp in my room was of brass with a pink porcelain shade, having airy figures in white. There were six tents, not counting the covered part set aside for [the] kitchen. The little canvas city was built upon a knoll that sloped up on three sides, and at the back, continued its rise into a high hill covered with fine trees — redwood, oak, madrone, and manzanita.

To secure good water, that greatest need in life, I had the water from a spring conveyed to our kitchen through three thousand feet of iron pipe, and two refrigerators kept food and water at the right temperature.

We had a number of hammocks swung in shady places, also swinging chairs suspended from large frames that I had built. One of our summer successes was an adjustable swinging chair that could be altered most easily by the foot of the occupant so as to enable him to take any position from the erect to the horizontal. There was a movable canopy over the entire framework and the whole affair was portable.

We found that a sort of enchanted, Arabian Nights effect was produced by our having about two hundred Chinese lanterns hanging from different heights of trees and flag-staff, and lighted every evening by the time we came out from dinner. The soft light thrown upon the dark foliage of the oaks, deepened where clusters of mistletoe had, here and there, found a lodgment, and the gentle breeze swinging the lanterns certainly were restful and exquisite, and kept us out in the sweet air generally until bed-time had sounded from the dear little cathedral clock that accompanies me when I travel.

Phoebe Apperson Hearst, correspondence, circa 1891, from the George and Phoebe Apperson Hearst Papers

Camp portrait, undated, from High Sierras Album

Now, this pillow is essential to comfort, and very simple. It is half a yard of muslin, sewed up as a bag, and filled with moss or hemlock browse. You can empty it and put it in your pocket, where it takes up about as much room as a handkerchief. You have other little muslin bags — an' you be wise.

"Nessmuk," *Woodcraft* (New York: Forest and Stream Publishing Co., 1884)

George Washington Sears borrowed his pen name "Nessmuk" (wood drake) from a young Narragansett Indian in Massachusetts who had befriended him and taught him to fish and camp. Sears was a frequent contributor to Forest and Stream *magazine in the 1880s.*

As we advanced northward, we began to get the wind very fresh in our faces, charged with the spray thrown up by the surf beating against miles of broken rock and solid wall that bound the shore for a long way above us. What with the slow start, the frequent changes, the visit at the rancho and the stopping to look at seals occasionally, the afternoon was pretty well worn away by the time we had traveled twenty miles; and the Captain proposed that we should go into camp at the first locality that offered us the requisites of wood, water, grass, and a lee. We reached such a one about four o'clock. It was a narrow valley between two considerable hills, opening seaward, over cliffs eighty or ninety feet in height, and landward, up into the stern, sterile mountains that come down here in a sharp spur from the coast range. The entire valley was not more than two acres in extent, and covered with a luxuriant growth of wild oats. We alighted, and in half an hour had a generous fire blazing before us, with a thick clump of shrubs at our backs, which were also almost a roof for us. I had never camped before; Geordie had, in crossing the Isthmus [of Panama]; so the edge of the novelty was taken off to her; but we felt such an escape from the care and labor that had borne so heavily upon us at home, and enjoyed so keenly the old holiday feeling that lights those rare seasons in childhood, that we did not require the stimulus of novelty to make us happy.

The event of the evening, after the horses were staked out, the fire made, and the blankets spread, was dinner. Good Miss Sampson had roasted, carved, and packed those moral antipodes, Dombey and Toots, in two small jars. We had a ham, bread, butter, cakes, nuts, raisins, brandy-peaches, and last our turnips and radishes, not the least desirable of our stores. It was first proposed to dine upon two courses; but there seemed a certain prodigality in this which prudence discouraged, so we agreed to disembowel one of the jars, and reserve the ham till next day. Mr. Toots was accordingly produced, and portions of him served on the small tin plates, which constituted the chief part of our dinner-service; but he had fared so hardly in life — having been the fag of the entire poultry-yard, and the unhappy recipient of so much (fowl) treatment — that, after the first few morsels, the flavor was voted bilious, and the ham taken in his stead.

This was really nice; and as we sat about the warm, bright fire, and saw the chill mist driving over the hills before us, and heard the surf madly chafing at the foot of the rocks, we felt much of the cozy comfort of a snug home. As the night threatened to be damp, and I was mentally wondering how Geordie and I were to sleep with nothing between us and the fog that occasionally shook out his gray wing, and again folded it, revealing momentary glimpses of blue sky and golden clouds, far above us, our Captain threw out some hints about the practicability of making a house that should serve us for a shelter. We liked not to be too earnest in commendation of the proposal, lest the difficulty should prove greater than it seemed to be; but he assured us that nothing could be easier, there being a small axe, plenty of boughs near at hand, and among us all an abundant supply of blankets to cover it with. When dinner was fairly over, both gentlemen set themselves diligently to work, and in a short time we were completely sheltered from both wind and fog in a little lodge, which, though of small dimensions, quite sufficed us all for a sitting-room during the evening, and Geordie and me for a sleeping-chamber and dressing-room. It was larger than our state-rooms at sea had been; and though we could not stand over four-and-a-half feet in it, we could sit very comfortably *à la Turque;* while, by the light of the great fire, I read the *Chronicles of Clovernook,* what time the hills resounded to shouts of laughter, and the seals on the rocks responded in an occasional bellow, as if the Land of Turveytop were a familiar country to them, and the Asyoulikeans old friends, whom they were glad to hear of again.

We read till a late hour; then we talked till a later one, inspired by the incomparable book — by the novelty of our situation — by the stern majesty of the darkness which brooded over us, and let loose the wings of thought, and unsealed the fountains of memory — so that the life of the past seemed to have compressed itself into those hours. At last, Geordie intimated a wish to go to rest, whereupon the gentlemen, having renewed the fire, betook themselves to their blankets and saddles, and in five minutes she was as sound asleep as if she had been at La Libertad in our own chamber. I could not sleep! A very long time had elapsed since my spirit had unfolded so free a pinion as it did that night.

[The next day] the Captain had dashed out a few yards ahead, when suddenly he pulled up, with the cry of "here they are, and plenty of them," and the next moment was half knee deep in a sand knoll covered with strawberry vines.

Eliza Woodson Farnham, *California In-doors and Out* (New York: Dix, Edwards, 1856)

On May 31, 1851, accompanied by two gentlemen, Richard Bruce and Mr. G, Eliza Farnham and her friend Georgiana "Geordie" Kirby left the potato farm and house they were building in Santa Cruz for a camping trip up the coast to pick strawberries. Both Farnham and Kirby were lifelong writers, feminists, and activists for education and prison reform.

"A camp site on the desert,"
Death Valley Automobile Trip, 1926

Summer tent, Napa County (?), circa 1905,
from the Wilson Family Papers

Kenwood Camp Stool advertisement in *Harper's Weekly,* March 25, 1893

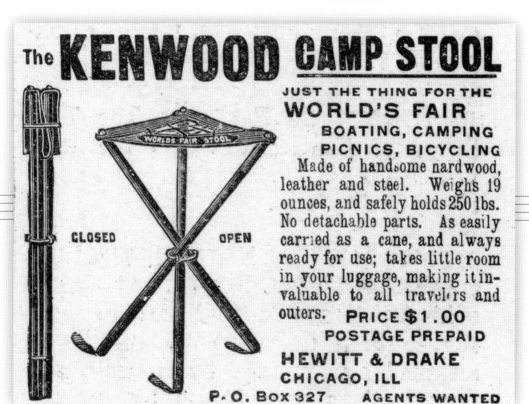

"View from the South," Merry Tramps of
Oakland, Sonoma County, California, 1886,
from the Frank B. Rodolph Photograph
Collection

White Mountain Hammock-Chair
advertisement in *Harper's Weekly*,
June 5, 1886

As we rode up through the trees, we felt that we had found an ideal place to camp. Down the mountain to the south you looked off on the blue ridges of the Coast Mountains, and above, the snow dome of Shasta. . . . It was indeed an ideal site for a camp, just inside a grove of firs 100–125 feet high and 2–4 feet in diameter with a clear cold mountain brook running just outside, and beyond it a meadow of ferns—brakes—brightened with blue flax, scarlet penstamons and red tiger lilies from the midst of which you looked up on the white peak. At the back of the camp were the two tents. A huge pine log walled the camp on the lower edge and served for hanging saddle blankets, pack saddles, harnesses, hobbles, grain bags, and other useful articles. Through the middle of the camp lay another log which in the daytime took the place of chairs and along which at night were unrolled a line of sleeping bags spread on balsam bough mattresses—tents are used only as dressing rooms for no one would have missed the opportunity to sleep out under the sky. Saddles, bridles, spurs, cameras, canteens, and cartridge belts hung on the trees while the guns stood against the trunks. Three hammocks and a swing for the children hung high from the great firs and gave a home-like air to the camp. And one end of the central log was upholstered with balsam boughs making a comfortable sofa back from which to watch the campfire before it. On the upper edge of camp the Chinaman made a cabin for himself in quite an ingenious manner. With the tree for a back, he drove two outer stakes and made what looked like a child's play house, making walls of boughs and a pair of chenille curtains he had brought and lining the whole with white muslin and putting in a bough bed.

. . . Dining room and kitchen were on the upper edge of camp. A log spread with white oilcloth served for dining table and the kitchen was conveniently near. A flat piece of sheet iron with round holes for covers was raised on stones and did well for frying and broiling but the ingenious Chinese cook did not approve of bake-oven biscuits so he made a regular oven in which he could bake bread and toast meat as well as on a stove. The oven was conical, about three feet high, like those made by the Mexicans. His was made entirely of mud and stones, and for draught had condensed milk cans in the top as chimneys. Our refrigerator was the brook, . . . but though this pantry was most convenient it had its disadvantages, for Jack the mule, in tramping about one day, discovered the jar and ate up all the butter.

Florence Merriam Bailey, "Camping on Mt. Shasta," 1898,
Florence Merriam Bailey Papers

Florence Merriam became half of a pioneering naturalist couple when she married Vernon Bailey in 1899. Together they made extensive trips into the American West where little was known about the flora and fauna; he focused on the mammals and she on the birds. She wrote stories and kept diaries about their varied camping experiences and authored Handbook of Birds of the Western United States *in 1902 and* Birds of New Mexico *in 1928.*

"San Francisco Boys' Outing Farm," near Saratoga, California, circa 1906, from the Alice Iola Hare Photograph Collection

Bertha Rice organized the Boys' Outing Farm near Saratoga, California, for city children orphaned by the 1906 San Francisco earthquake.

[In 1896] We picked a camping spot in the middle of the [Yosemite] Valley and made camp in a grove of small trees right on the river. Our camp was completely hidden from the road by thick brush. We fixed up a fine camp and as a finishing touch put out our American flag which turned out to be a mistake. The flag was all right, but the camp was not, and brought the Ranger down on us to tell us that it was against all rules of the park to camp anyplace except in the prescribed camping grounds. We were just eating lunch and he gladly accepted an invitation to join us. After a bountiful repast and a couple of helpings of cake he said if we took the flag down no one would notice the place and he guessed it would be OK. He enjoyed his meal so much he found it necessary to inspect our camp on every chance possible — at meal time. His name was Percy, I think, and he helped us a lot.

Adolph D. Sweet, "Down a Glacier a Mile a Minute," *Tulare County Historical Society Bulletin* No. 7, March 1951, Visalia, California

Toward this point we directed our course, marching wearily over stretches of dense frozen snow, and regions of *débris*, reaching about sunset the last alcove of the amphitheater, just at the foot of the Mount Brewer wall. It was evidently impossible for us to attempt to climb it that evening, and we looked about the desolate recesses for a sheltered camping-spot. A high granite wall surrounded us upon three sides, recurring to the southward in long elliptical curves; no part of the summit being less than two thousand feet above us, the higher crags not unfrequently reaching three thousand feet. A single field of snow swept around the base of the rock and covered the whole amphitheater, except where a few spikes and rounded masses of granite rose through it, and where two frozen lakes, with their blue ice-disks, broke the monotonous surface. Through the white snow-gate of our amphitheater, as through a frame, we looked eastward upon the summit group; not a tree, not a vestige of vegetation in sight — sky, snow, and granite the only elements in the wild picture. After searching for a shelter we at last found a granite crevice near the margin of one of the frozen lakes — a sort of shelf just large enough for [Richard] Cotter and me — where we hastened to make our bed, having first filled the canteen from a small stream that trickled over the ice, knowing that in a few moments the rapid chill would freeze it. We ate our supper of cold venison and bread, and whittled from the sides of the wooden barometer-case shavings enough to warm water for a cup of miserably tepid tea, and then, packing our provisions and instruments away at the head of the shelf, rolled ourselves in our blankets and lay down to enjoy the view. After such fatiguing exercises the mind has an almost abnormal clearness: whether this is wholly from within, or due to the intensely vitalizing mountain air, I am not sure; probably both contribute to the state of exaltation in which all alpine climbers find themselves. The solid granite gave me a luxurious repose, and I lay on the edge of our little rock niche and watched the strange yet brilliant scene.

Clarence King, *Mountaineering in the Sierra Nevada* (Boston: J. R. Osgood and Co., 1872)

As a young geologist and mountaineer, Clarence King was invited by William Brewer and Josiah Whitney to join the California Geological Survey. He later became the founder and first director of the U.S. Geological Survey.

Summer camp of Dr. John Robertson's family
and Ambrose Bierce, Arroyo del Valle, near
Livermore, California, July 4, 1898, from
the Marjorie Robertson Grabhorn Papers
in the Bancroft Portrait Collection

Interior of Tents—Noyo River Tavern,
California Scenic Line, circa 1900

**Produced by the California Western
Railroad & Navigation Company line,
which runs from the coastal town of
Fort Bragg through the redwood forests
of Mendocino County to Willits, California, this promotional album includes
photographs of the Noyo River Tavern,
a railroad resort near the tracks.**

Palmetto Tents,
advertisement in
Harper's Weekly,
July 7, 1877

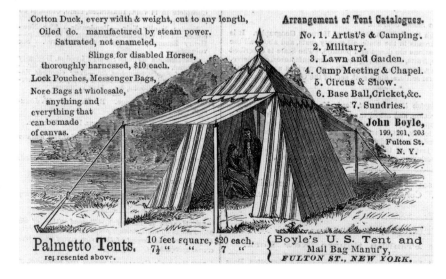

"Camping at Mt. Shasta,"
July 1888, from the Frank
B. Rodolph Photograph
Collection

Two-Way Tent
"With or Without Center Pole"

TWO-WAY TENT
"WITH OR WITHOUT CENTER POLE"

The "TWO-WAY" Tent has been designed by BROOKS to fill the demand for a square tent without center pole. Most—if not all—of the many previous attempts at such a tent have been impractical because they entailed much labor in handling the tent in camp and excessive weight and bulk in carrying.

In the "TWO-WAY" Tent these objections have been overcome and BROOKS has developed at a LOW PRICE a light, compact, practical tent, easily and quickly put up and taken down by ONE person, with no center pole to obstruct the space inside the tent. All work of erection is accomplished from OUTSIDE the tent.

Should use of this tent WITH a center pole be desired, three bottom sections of the steel tubing frame can be utilized for the pole. There is a collapsible wooden frame in the eaves of the tent which remains in place at all times and folds up with the tent.

The "TWO-WAY" Tent is constructed of durable, efficient rainproof green cloth, drill weave, weighing 8.16 ozs. per square yard in the grey. Awning lowers to form the wide cloth door. Both door and large rear window are equipped with bobbinet screens. The window also has a cloth storm flap. BROOKS Quality Materials and Workmanship throughout. Floor is of duck weighing 8.69 ozs. per square yard in the grey, khaki color, water and mildew treated, sewed to tent.

The frame supporting the "TWO-WAY" Tent is of steel tubing and stands entirely on the OUTSIDE of the tent, as shown in the accompanying illustration. This permits erection without entering the tent and avoids the unpleasant task of crawling underneath the folds of the tent while on the ground in order to start erection.

The "TWO-WAY" Tent is made in TWO REGULAR SIZES. The height at center is 7 ft. 8 ins.; at the eaves, 6 ft. 2 ins. These tents are 4½ ft. square at the eaves. The "clear space" afforded by the outside frame makes this an unusually roomy tent. Each tent complete with sewed-in canvas floor, including steel stakes. One color only—dark green waterproof material.

ONE PACKAGE—Rolls in one package, 8 ins. by 54 ins.

No. 379—Two-Way Tent. Size, 7x9 feet. Net weight, 42 lbs.; shipping weight, 47 lbs. Price, each. **$22.25**

No. 399—Two-Way Tent. Size 9½x9½ feet. Net weight, 45 lbs.; shipping weight, 50 lbs. Price, each. **24.50**

The Rival Umbrella Tent

ADJUSTABLE UMBRELLA ARMS WITH PATENTED CLAMP ON TWO PIECE CENTER POLE

STORM PROOF WINDOW 18 X 20

Our low-priced Umbrella Tent. Made of khaki waterproofed tent duck (weighing 7.45 ozs. per square yard in the grey), weighing 10 ozs. per square yard after waterproofing. Sewed-in floor of khaki waterproofed tent duck (of same weight as tent). Steel umbrella arms fit into sewed-in rings at corners. Patented clamp holds umbrella arms in position on 2-piece wood center pole. Large screened window in rear, 18x20 inches, with storm flap operated from inside of tent. Awning equipped with strings so that when let down to form a door it can be securely tied. Has canvas loops at corners and sides to receive stakes. Height at center, 7 ft. 6 ins.; eaves, 6 ft. high and 4 ft. 6 ins. wide. Door opening is 29 ins. wide and 6 ft. high. Has sewed-in floor, bobbinet door with tie strings attached and 7-in. door riser to keep out insects. Tent is complete for use. Equipment includes sewed-in floor, bobbinet door, umbrella arms with center pole, wood tent stakes and guy ropes for awning. Awning poles not included. Tent and poles roll into a bundle 8 ins. in diameter and 43 ins. long.

Made in three popular sizes as shown below:

No. 207—Size, 7x 7 ft.; weight, 40 lbs. Price, each. **$17.80**
No. 209—Size, 7x 9½ ft.; weight, 45 lbs. Price, each. **19.85**
No. 211—Size, 9x11 ft.; weight, 55 lbs. Price, each. **23.65**

Popular "Lean To" Style Auto Tents

The Overland Tourist Tent

The Overland Tourist Tent is made in three sizes and two materials as listed. Light in weight and compact to carry. May be used with the automobile or separate from the automobile, as illustrated. Complete with ropes and stakes. Carrying sack furnished with each tent.

NET PRICES

No.	Size, Ft.	Height	Wall	10 oz. Stand. White Duck (9.93 oz. per Sq. Yd.)	Weight Lbs.	7-45 Khaki Waterproofed Duck (Grey Wgt.)	Weight Lbs.
45	5 x7	6'0"	2'0"	$ 6.60 ea.	12	$ 7.25 ea.	18
47	7 x7	6'0"	2'0"	8.15 ea.	15	8.95 ea.	22
49	9½ x7	6'0"	2'0"	9.60 ea.	18	10.90 ea.	27

No poles are furnished with this tent. Awning may be used to close front of tent or as an awning. Rope full length of ridge to front guys.
See page 12 for price on poles.

The Yellowstone Touring Tent

INDEPENDENT OF AUTOMOBILE, USING POLES

This tent is made in two sizes only and two materials as listed. The partition between the tent and awning adds to the comfort of this tent. May be used with the automobile or separate from the automobile by use of poles as illustrated. No ridge pole required, as side guy ropes are a continuous rope running through the ridge of the tent. Light and compact to carry. Carrying sack of same material furnished with each tent.

No poles are furnished with this tent. Ropes and stakes included with each tent. Carrying sack of same material. Rope full length of ridge to front guys.

See page 12 for price on poles.

TENT ATTACHED TO CAR - TWO POLES USED

NET PRICES

No.	Size, Ft.	Height	Wall	10 oz. Stand. White Duck (9.93 oz. per Sq. Yd.)	Weight Lbs.	7-45 Khaki Waterproofed Duck (Grey Wgt.)	Weight Lbs.
37	7 x7	6'6"	3'0"	$11.55 ea.	20	$12.70 ea.	30
39	9½x7	6'6'	3'0"	14.20 ea.	25	15.60 ea.	38

Catalog No. 35, The Brooks Tent and Awning Company,
April 1, 1935, Denver, Colorado

"Grandma's Tent, July 4, 1887," from the Frank B. Rodolph Photograph Collection

"Wells Flat," circa 1900, from
the Lohry Family Photographs

Sunday we dressed up in our mountain rig and all got in one room and looked at each other and talked mountain slang as near as we could. We all felt new and looked more so. A genuine back-woodsman would have been greatly amused had he been where he could hear us talk. A big knife at our side, a pistol in our belt, and a magazine gun in our hands, long boots, our pants in the legs, blue shirts and big white straw hats, all new and we ourselves the newest of all. I think I can never forget our appearance on that Sunday afternoon, how we did talk about killing deer, cougar, and all other varmints. Alas, poor fellows, little did we know what we were talking about.

James Wilson, "A Trip in the Cascade Mountains," 1883, manuscript

This trip was taken "with the view of ascertaining what real rough life in the mountains was like." The campers were a group of five San Franciscans and the two young sons of one of them. "We had great hardships and but little real pleasure, but each returned well pleased and with a possible hope of some day going off again."

"Lunch by the roadside near Water's Ranch," Big Sur, California, June 7, 1927;
Charles Fremont Pond; Elizabeth Keith Pond Mountain Journals, Keith-McHenry-Pond Family Papers

Near Petrolia we made a fine camp in a grassy meadow. Green snakes appeared at nearly every step, but what cared we! At sundown along came the cattle; many coming right into camp to inspect us, but we make friends with all the creatures great and small. Three horses awoke me at dawn, hanging right over me, breathing and snorting at the strange bundle on the ground in their pasture! We have slept with the pigs too! The country dogs are very friendly, and all, pigs, sheep, and cattle, are very grateful for a little petting.

Elizabeth Keith Pond, Mountain Journal IV, Humboldt County, June 21, 1921, Keith-McHenry-Pond Family Papers

Campsite, Glenwood, 1900

WEIGHS LESS THAN 10 LBS

PERFECTION MATTRESS

ALWAYS DRY AND COMFORTABLE.

AIR -NOT- HAIR

IS THE MODERN FILLING FOR MATTRESSES AND CUSHIONS.

AIR PUMP

PERFECTION CUSHION

PLEASURES OF CAMPING may be increased many fold by using "PERFECTION" Air Mattresses and Cushions, the most comfortable made. *Waterproof—Light—Convenient.* Yachtsmen should investigate. *Send for illustrated catalogue.* MECHANICAL FABRIC CO., Air-Goods Department, Providence, R. I.

[We] **D**ragged our sleeping bags well out into the middle of the dry pumice slope. Before retiring we picked out the largest of the stones from our sandy bed, then spread our bags. Though the pumice slope sounded hard, it really made the best bed we had during the six weeks that we slept on the ground on Shasta, for the sand conformed to the topographical features of our frames enough to relieve the hard monotony of an absolutely level surface. In the night, bats would often fly so low over our bags that we could hear their wings close above our faces. As we lay, composing ourselves for slumber, across the meadow the big yellow moon would rise between the fir spires, glowing brighter and brighter till it shone full into camp, whitening our tents and actually making us turn away from the intensity of its light.

Florence Merriam Bailey, "Camping on Mt. Shasta," 1898, from the Florence Merriam Bailey Papers

"Air Not Hair," Perfection Mattresses advertisement in *Harper's Weekly,* July 9, 1898

In the cove there is a small sandy beach, upon which the waves have drifted and deposited a large quantity of oat-straw, and feathers shed by the millions of water-fowls which sport upon the bay. On this downy deposit furnished by nature, we spread our blankets, and slept soundly.

Edwin Bryant, *What I Saw in California* (New York: D. Appleton & Company, 1848)

So sometime after noon we drove into a grove of trees and camped on the bank of a good-sized stream, probably the Stanislaus River. After a gloomy consult, we decided to sleep on the soft side of a sandy bank. That night was a memorable one. Never having slept on a sand bank before, I was wholly unprepared to find how hard just ordinary soft-looking sand can become when trying to use it for a mattress!"

Catherine Norton Case, "Priest's Grade and Big Oak Flat in 1860," 1905, manuscript

I made my bed in a nook of the pine-thicket, where the branches were pressed and crinkled over-head like a roof, and bent down around the sides. These are the best bedchambers the high mountains afford — snug as squirrel-nests, well ventilated, full of spicy odors, and with plenty of wind-played needles to sing one asleep. I little expected company, but, creeping in through a low side-door, I found five or six birds nestling among the tassels.

John Muir, *The Mountains of California* (New York, The Century Co., 1894)

It is from this tree, called Red Fir by the lumberman, that mountaineers always cut boughs to sleep on when they are so fortunate as to be within its limits. Two rows of the plushy branches over-lapping along the middle, and a cres-cent of smaller plumes mixed with ferns and flowers for a pillow, form the very best bed imaginable. The essences of the pressed leaves seem to fill every pore of one's body, the sounds of falling water make a soothing hush, while the spaces between the grand spires afford noble openings through which to gaze dream-ily into the starry sky. Even in the mat-ter of sensuous ease, any combination of cloth, steel springs, and feathers seems vulgar in comparison.

John Muir, "The Coniferous Forests of the Sierra Nevada," in *Scribner's Monthly*, October 1881

The bedding (weighing less than ten pounds) consists of a large eiderdown quilt, on one side covered by a sheet of the lightest calico, of a color which will not crock; on the other by a sheet of light but firm tan-color canvas, both sheets merely basted on with strong thread. Along the edges and bottom of the canvas strong tapes are firmly sewed at intervals of a foot or less in opposite pairs, so that they can be tied together when it is desired to turn the quilt into a sleeping-bag. There is a great advantage in this on a warm night; for the heat becomes intolerable in a close bag; but this can be alleviated by untying the tapes and allowing the cooling air to enter. Instead of tapes, large safety-pins might be used, but they are liable to be lost, while the tapes, if well sewed to the canvas, will last as long as the bag. Upon the return from the trip I always rip off the calico and have it washed, remove the canvas, cover the quilt with cheese-cloth, and use it again on the bed. The bag when rolled for packing is protected by a canvas flap twenty-eight inches by nineteen, the longer dimension being sewed to the middle of the canvas at the top of the quilt. This flap is also fine for covering the head at night. Two or three long double tapes are sewed to the free edge of the flap. When it is desired to pack the bedding, the two long edges of the quilt are brought together along the middle of the quilt, then the folded quilt is rolled from the bottom up as tightly as possible, and the flap rolled around and tied by the tapes, one of each pair being turned in one direction and the other in the opposite, so that they may be tied firmly together.

Alice Eastwood, "Description of a Light, Compact Arrangement of Bedding and Personal Effects for a Camping-Trip," in the *Sierra Club Bulletin,* vol. 5, no. 1, January 1904

Self-taught Canadian botanist Alice Eastwood was curator at the California Academy of Sciences herbarium in San Francisco from 1892 to 1949.

Our beds were made of fresh hay; on the hay were piled many layers of hemlock boughs — the soft outer ends; one gets critical of quality in tree boughs as bedding; then new uncut blue blankets were unrolled and laid full length across the high elastic pile where we were to sleep in a long row, Hannah, myself, and the children, with little "Fan" as postscript. It was so high a pile we had to take it with a running jump. The men's camp was off by the spring and where smoke would not blow toward us.

Jessie Benton Frémont, *Far-West Sketches* (Boston: D. Lothrop Co., 1890)

The wife of explorer John Frémont, Jessie Benton Frémont began her writing career by helping her husband write the reports of his exploits for the United States government. She later helped to support the family by publishing her own reminiscences.

There are a great many very competent treatises telling you how to build your fire, pitch your tent, and all the rest of it. I have never seen described the woodsmen's method of using a blanket, however. Lie flat on your back. Spread the blanket over you. Now raise your legs rigid from the hip, the blanket of course draping over them. In two swift motions tuck first one edge under your legs from right to left, then the second edge under from left to right, and over the first edge. Lower your legs, wrap up your shoulders, and go to sleep. If you roll over, one edge will unwind but the other will tighten.

Stewart Edward White, *Camp and Trail* (New York: The Outing Publishing Co., 1907)

"Ranger's Camp, The Awakening, Kings River Canyon," 1929, from the Joseph N. LeConte Photograph Collection

"Glenola Behling Rose, Robert E. Rose, 1938," from the Agnes Fay Morgan papers

Glenola Rose and Agnes Morgan were fellow chemists who specialized in nutrition in order to excel in their male-dominated field.

THREE

Pastimes

Hammocks and rope swings aided campers intent on spending their stays in the wild with their feet up. Dime novels were easily tucked into knapsacks and brought out after the morning mush residue had been sanded out of the frying pan. There were fish to catch, and miner's lettuce and various berries to pick, wood to gather, tents to stake, and socks to wash, but also hikes, swimming holes, lovely landscapes, and the general all-around conviviality that is part and parcel of camp trappings. And in the evenings, as the perfect darkness settled in, there were songs, skits, and stories around the campfire to complete the day.

"The Mott children at camp" near Santa Rosa,
New Mexico, 1903; Florence Merriam Bailey;
from the Vernon Bailey Collection

"The noon hour: Oliver, Parker, and Hicks resting," near Calistoga, California, 1898, University of California, Berkeley, Summer School of Surveying, from the Oliver Family Photograph Collection

Laid 'round camp all day. Was too tired to clamber up any more mountains today. Frank went fishing. I hitched up, haul'd some firewood, then we drove down to the Gallery, had some views taken of ourselves and outfit, with the Yo Semite in the background, then drove back to camp and played "California Jack" and went out and killed a few squirrels.

Diary entry, Frank B. Rodolph, Saturday, May 19, 1877, manuscript

Tuesday, June 11. We arrived at the Great Tunnel and Big Trees of Tuolumne at 6 o'clock, and pitched camp after supper. I entertained myself with cornet playing, the tones of which re-echoed through the canyon. We camped on a side hill facing one of the great trees of the grove. We were awakened in the morning by our horses, they having gotten away. George Schultz ran for over a mile with only his draws on, and finally caught them.

Alonzo Coffin, "An Account of an Excursion to Yosemite Valley, June 1 to June 23, 1895," manuscript

Coffin was the owner of California Pattern Works in San Francisco. One of his tentmates was Albert Ogg, who also kept a journal of the trip.

"Dr. Ray," Larkspur Canyon, Mt. Tamalpais, Marin County, California, 1904, Family Album of San Jose and San Francisco Bay Area Views

"The Grey Rock Quartette, Giant Forest," "Patsey," Helen Greame, Alicia Mosgrove, Dr. Marian Hooker, Katherine Bunnell, Kings Canyon, California, 1902, from the Francis P. Farquhar Photograph Collection

CROQUET GROUND — NOYO RIVER TAVERN

California Scenic
Line Photograph
Album, circa 1900.
Croquet Ground,
Noyo River Tavern

George W. Ames camp at Ibex,
Photographs from a Trip in Death Valley, July 1915

Swim in the Cold Soda Spring Wee Wa (little Warren) takes a dive

Nona and I took Mollie Woolsey down to our "Azalea Bath" as we call it, and we treated ourselves to a delicious bath. We were now more used to the water and could stay in a longer time. "Azalea Bath" was fit for a queen. A circle of rocks so guarded the sheltered cove that there was not the least current; the clear soft ripples lapped gently on a shelving beach; sugar pines and firs shaded the banks and fragrant azaleas wove a curtain.

Camp diary, Caroline Eaton LeConte, Yosemite, June 1878, LeConte Family Papers

"Little Joe" LeConte's older sister Caroline was fourteen when she kept this illustrated diary of a family camping trip.

"Swim in the Cold Soda Spring, Wee Wa (little Warren) takes a dive," Clear Lake, California, June 1924; Charles Fremont Pond; Elizabeth Keith Pond Mountain Journals, Keith-McHenry-Pond Family Papers

"On with the dance! Let Joy be unconfined!"
from "A Souvenir of Camp 'Robin Hood,'"
Lake Traverse, Minnesota, July 1900

March 11. Arrived at the Sentinel Hotel at 7 p.m., having come about twelve miles. Found three or four inches of soft snow in the Valley. I would have given a good deal for a hot tub, but Charlie dissuaded me from any such luxury, as we expected to go out the next day and must keep hard and taut for the snow-shoeing. Up in the high country in winter there is no dust and everything keeps clean; the skin needs little bathing and keeps soft and firm with bacon grease. And camp-fire smoke!

Elizabeth Keith Pond, Mountain
Journal II, Yosemite, March 1912,
Keith-McHenry-Pond Family Papers

And the rapture of mere solo bathing in soft cold mountain water has never been sufficiently sung. Those emerald, those aquamarine floods are soft and soothing as chilled velvet, exhilarating as sparkling light. As a small child I used to play with a boy named "Bill," who had an ill-concealed contempt for the weaker sex as he knew it. At the age of eleven, he wrote a poem setting forth the disadvantages of girls. I remember two withering lines:

"They cannot climb up trees for fruit,
Nor bathe without a bathing-suit."

Across the years we salute you, Bill, and tell you times have changed.

Bertha Clark Pope, "The High Trip of 1925," in the *Sierra Club Bulletin*, vol. 12, no. 3, 1926

Between Sierra Club outings, Bertha Pope edited the Letters of Ambrose Bierce *in 1922.*

"The Bathroom," Selina Solomons at Steven's Creek, Santa Clara County, California, circa 1888, from Views of Camping in California

Suffragist and author of *How We Won the Vote* in 1911, Selina Solomons was the younger sister of Theodore Solomons, explorer and cartographer of Yosemite.

Nacimiento River, Saturday Afternoon, May 4, 1861 — I returned from a long walk at noon and concluded to devote the afternoon to writing and "chores." First, dinner; next, put on clean clothes and wash my dirty ones. . . . First, I get a place on the bank and begin. A huge gust scatters sand over the wet clothes, which are in a pile on the bank. Stockings are washed — I congratulate myself on how well I have done it. An undershirt is begun — goes on swimmingly. Suddenly the sand close to the water where I squat gives way. I go in, half boot deep, and in the strife to get out, tread on the clean stockings and shove them three inches into the mud and sand. A stick is got and laid close to the water. On that I kneel, as do the Mexican and Indian washerwomen. This goes better, and the work goes bravely on. Next, the slippery soap glides out of my hands and into the deep water — here a long delay in poking it out with a long stick, during which performance it goes every way except toward shore. At last the final garment is washed. With a long breath I rise to leave, when I find the lowest of the clean pile is all dirty from the log I laid them on — the cleanest place I could find. But soon all difficulties are surmounted, and the clothes are now fluttering in the wind, suspended from one of the guy ropes of our tent. The picture is underdrawn rather than exaggerated — just try it by taking your clothes to the creek to wash the next time.

William H. Brewer, *Up and Down California in 1860–1864,* edited by Francis P. Farquhar (Berkeley: University of California Press, 1932)

A prolific diarist and correspondent, and a member of the Geological Survey of California from 1860 to 1864, Brewer described his Western campsites in great detail and humor, while maintaining the records of the Survey's botanical collections.

"Palache scrubbing socks — washing socks in the bread pan," from a diary entry by Joseph N. LeConte, Hetch Hetchy and Yosemite trip, 1889, from the LeConte Family Papers

Wash dishes at once after finishing a meal. It is easier and will soon be over. Use sand or leaves to remove grease. Paper will assist also. Firewood ashes make excellent scouring material. Have a flat rock, box, or hewed log to put knives, pots, pans, and kettles on. An old wives' tale is that if soot burns around the rocks or in the fireplace it will rain in twenty-four hours. Be sure to put things back in their places or they will be lost. Do not leave anything on the ground.

George Bird Grinnell and Dr. Eugene L. Swan, eds., *Harper's Camping and Scouting; An Outdoor Guide for American Boys* (New York: Harper & Bros., 1907)

The Camp Cobbler

"The Camp Cobbler," in Ford A. Carpenter's "Springtime in the High Sierra; A Record of Journeyings with the Sierra Club," July–August 1901, Sierra Club Photograph Albums

last nights sleeping system would not fulfill the purpose, and so we moved our provisions out in the threatening weather and put George in their place, Vernon in George's place, leaving me in my place, the front seat. Everybody slept well but George, who was somewhat cramped by his position.

Feb 8 (Sunday) Dawned fairly fair. We found we had been sleeping next to the sewage disposal system, and decided that we would not breakfast there, but a little way down the river by the little fall we passed yesterday morning. The "little way down the River proved some four miles, much to our delight, but

was a pretty good place, at that.

We hauled out the stove, and had breakfast cooking in no time. The picture shows Geo. & Vernon doing their bit while I record it for future generations. Our quarters were supplied by running water, seen in the background. A dozen eggs, 2 quarts of chocolate, and a half pound of bacon furnished our meagre breakfast. We ate so much that George suggested that we climb the first little step of the falls there. So we forged upward, and were delighted by the

Diary entry, David Brower, Yosemite, February 8, 1931, from the David Ross Brower Papers

Brower devoted many daylight hours to his camp diaries, which include photographs, pressed flowers, and lists of ingredients for some of his culinary exploits, such as mulligan stew made with oatmeal and cocoa. In the early days, though he was climbing peaks and traveling throughout the Sierra Nevada, he seemed to be moving from meal to meal rather than from mile to mile. His ever-present Sierra cup was the receptacle for all he ate and drank on the trail or in camp.

Chiura Obata, Sierra Club High Trip, North and South Forks of the San Joaquin River, 1938, Sierra Club Collection of Cedric Wright Photographs

Through art, Chiura Obata documented the experience of being a prisoner in a Japanese American internment camp during World War II. Fusing traditional Japanese sumi ink painting with the conventions of western naturalism, Obata was a master of his craft and an esteemed teacher. After his release, he camped and painted in the High Sierra.

Cedric Wright was first a concert violinist, then turned his musicality toward his camera, photographing the landscape as he camped.

Next morning was a winter morning. The day was half sunshine, half cloud, and the snow rapidly melted. It was curious to see the different colors of flowers peeping out from this white background, and at night we had a magnificent effect of sunset. The sky perfectly clear, patches of snow and snow shadow, sunlight on distant spire and cliff—great heavy sodden masses of cloud cutting off the tops of the mountain, square and rigid at the top, yet with a slow and solid motion at the bottom, broken up into a cloudy, foamy-like smoke, the foreground pines standing clear and sharp of a brilliant yellow green with the green fused into the yellow, as you see in a roaring campfire the fusion of orange, sulphur, and gold. I made a quick and hasty sketch which looked better next morning and watched the light throbbing fainter and fainter until lost in night.

William Keith, "An Artist's Trip in the Sierra," 1875, manuscript

William Keith was the leading artist in San Francisco at the end of the nineteenth century, called by John Muir a "poet-painter." Keith arrived at Muir's cabin in Yosemite Valley in 1872 with a letter of introduction and a lifelong friendship developed, during which they camped together in the High Sierra. This trip was taken in the company of John Swett, Mr. McChesney, and John Muir.

William Keith, poet Charles Keeler, essayist and
beloved observer of nature John Burroughs together
in Yosemite, 1896, Bancroft Portrait Collection

June 29th.... I went upstream a little to try
my luck [at fishing]. At first it seemed hope-
less, but then I struck a pool in which I could
see fish, and caught three. I only took along
4 flies, and one fish (3') got away, so I had to
come back for more bait. I caught more flies
in a surprising place and then, settling down
in a pool 100' from camp, I took 7 more, the
longest about 9". These 10 make a lifetime
total of 11. The other one, caught about 1924,
slipped through a hole in my pocket and no
one else ever saw it. However these 10 are right
in sight now, but will not be when tomorrow's
breakfast is over. I fished in my shorts, and the
backs of my legs were nicely burned, too nicely,
before I realized it and quit, to come in at 4:30
to eat lunch.

Diary entry, David Ross Brower, June 29, 1934,
David Ross Brower papers

When he was twenty-two, Brower went on a
seven-week camping and climbing trip in the
Sierra Nevada with his hometown Berkeley friend
George Rockwood, from June 15 to August 5, 1934.
They had little money to outfit themselves, but
energy and curiosity enough to improvise.

"13-lb. Salmon," Pyramid Lake, Nevada,
August 1927, Elizabeth Keith Pond Mountain
Journals, Keith-McHenry-Pond Family Papers

Trout stream _ "Sulphur creek," California.

"Trout Stream—
Sulphur Creek,
California," Galt,
circa 1855

Right here let me whisper a past master fisherman's secret—in order to gain the best results when all fashionable bait has failed, catch a fat and juicy grub worm, bite off his head before you place him on the hook; you may not fancy the taste on the start, but you will soon cultivate a liking when you note the results; if your angle-worm fails you at a critical moment, just spit tobacco juice all over him, put him back in the creek and you will be a winner.

Vernille DeWitt Warr, "A Woman in the Wilds" in *Western Field*, January 1912

"Helen Gompertz LeConte on Mt. Ritter, 13,143 feet, 1897," from the Joseph N. LeConte Photograph Collection

"Little Joe" LeConte's first wife, Helen, was a member of the first party to climb the Sierra Nevada's University Peak (13,632 feet), in 1896, and Split Mountain (14,058 feet), in 1902.

Virginia de Fremery, Kings River
Canyon, 1938, from the Sierra
Club Collection of Cedric Wright
Photographs

The Yo Semite is the most interesting place in the world. My plan is to go there about the middle of June, with ten friends, and stay three months. We must take trained saddle ponies, a good guide, and have a camp which we can move in and about the valley on the backs of mules. The party must be at least half ladies. I have found them more enthusiastic, more patient with hunger and hard climbing, and more plucky than men. When a spirited young woman gets off her long skirts and corsets, gets on a pair of mountain boots and strong gloves, with a short, strong dress, she will come as near to flying as anything human I have ever met. As to daring in ticklish places, men are nowhere.

Dio Lewis, M.D., *Gypsies, or Why We Went Gypsying in the Sierras* (Boston: Eastern Book Co., 1881)

After thirty years of "unbroken toil as a physician" in New York, Dr. Lewis went to the Pacific coast with a group of family and friends and "rested for three years" to restore his own health, camping throughout California.

July 23, 1889, Grand Canyon of the Tuolumne. We meditatively let our legs dangle over the edge of the amphitheatre, and, looking down into the abyss and counting the lakes and snow banks, we munched our cold leathery flapjacks, and crunched our snow. It was the coldest lunch I ever ate.

Diary entry, Joseph Nisbet LeConte, LeConte Family Papers

Muir Club, Girls' Outing, San Joaquin River and Evolution Basin, 1924, from the Leonarde Keeler Photograph Collection

"Nineteen-year-old whiz kid" mountain guide Leonarde Keeler learned to camp as a child in the hills near Calistoga. Later, as a criminologist working for the Berkeley Police Department, he made significant improvements to the polygraph machine.

"Mazamas on Mt. Pitt," (Mount McLoughlin, Jackson County),
Oregon, 1896, from the Vernon Bailey Collection

The Mazamas slogan is "We Climb High," and they have been doing that while
advocating preservation, exploration, and nature education since 1894.

Tommy Jefferson (?),
campfire, Sierra Club High
Trip to Yosemite, circa 1941,
from the Sierra Club Collection
of Cedric Wright Photographs

The night came on cold and wild, with clouds and wind and fitful moonlight. The guides built a campfire on the rocks, which we gathered about, and roasted our faces while our backs were shivering. The only chance of comfort would have been in continually revolving, by some sort of spit arrangement—to turn one's self was too much like work; yet we were very merry—not at all put down by little discomforts and great sublimities. Mr. Muir built large fires down by the river. The effects of the red gleams and wavering flashes among the rocks and dark pines, and of the reflections on the rapids, were marvelously picturesque.... We took to reciting ballads and telling stories. Of the latter, the most horrible and hair-elevating sort were at a premium. There was a generous and amiable strife as to who should contribute most to the general discomfort, and produce the most startling and blood-curdling effects.

Grace Greenwood, *New Life in New Lands: Notes of Travel* (New York: J. B. Ford and Co., 1873)

Journalist, author, and publisher under her pseudonym Grace Greenwood, Sarah Jane Lippincott was the first woman in the United States to become a regular newspaper correspondent. She was an outspoken advocate for women's rights, peace, prison reform, and the abolition of slavery and capital punishment.

"In fifteen minutes at most your meal is ready," illustration by Thomas Fogarty from Stewart Edward White's *The Forest* (New York: The Outlook Company, 1903)

Marion Randall Parsons making tea
on the summit of Liberty Cap; Edward
Taylor Parsons, photographer; Sierra
Club outing, Mt. Ritter, July 1909

FOUR

Hash and Ashcakes

Food always tastes better in camp than at home. You can boil up a mess of beans or stew some prunes, make biscuits, bacon, coffee, or flapjacks at home, but they won't taste anything like the way they do when cooked over a campfire. This was as true in the past as it is today, although notorious culinary fiascos happened, too. Recipes and hints for camp food were passed back and forth, including such specialties as dry camp cooking (use beer instead of water in your hotcake batter) and high altitude snacks (spoon strawberry jam onto snow). The regulars knew how to take advantage of local produce and scoffed at the novices, "Fool tourists missed the raspberries!"

Adams and
Westlake
Oil Stove
advertisement,
Harper's Weekly,
April 17, 1880

Making fire by friction of dry sticks is an art not often practiced in these days, but two Palm Springs Indians with whom I once camped were experts at the game. Two pieces of dry palm-fruit stem were the tools, one an inch or so broad, length immaterial, the other less than half as thick, about a foot long and perfectly straight. A few dead leaves were placed in a little heap: the larger stick was laid beside them and held in place by one of the men, a hollow having first been made in the surface of the wood, with a little groove leading from it to the leaves. Then the smaller stick, trimmed to a blunt point, was put to the hollow, and rapidly revolved by rolling between the open hands of the other Indian. His hands

moved down as he rolled, returning again and again to the top. The friction sent a fine stream of wood powder down the groove upon the leaves. In less than two minutes smoke showed at the point of friction, then sparks began to fall on the tinder, and finally a flame was started by blowing. Less than three minutes sufficed for the operation. It was hard work while it lasted, for the fire was endangered by the perspiration caused in kindling it.

J. Smeaton Chase, *California Desert Trails* (Boston and New York: Houghton Mifflin Co., 1919)

An easy-going, observant, and witty transplanted Englishman, photographer, author, and solo camper, Chase wore riding breeches, leather puttees, a brown tweed coat, and a broad-brimmed Stetson hat. With his packhorse "Kaweah," he camped throughout California, after learning to love the outdoor life during a period of frugality in the hills around San Diego necessitated when his inheritance was lost in a bank failure.

To dry matches: Carefully blot off as much water as possible with a soft cloth and then pass them through the hair a dozen times or so.

Handbook for Campers in the National Forests in California, U.S. Department of Agriculture, Forest Service (Washington, D.C.: Government Printing Office, 1915)

A very convenient, easily prepared and efficient fire starter for the use of the camper ... in forest or mountain is simply a can of sawdust saturated with kerosene. Provided that reasonably dry wood be used, a tablespoonful of this will start a fire quickly.

Norman Clyde, "A Convenient and Efficient Fire Starter," undated, Norman Clyde Papers

Clyde also suggested using cotton balls soaked in petroleum jelly.

Sierra Club High Trip stove chimneys, circa 1946, from the Sierra Club Collection of Cedric Wright Photographs

The new Dutch-oven, primarily intended for the baking of bread, came to fulfill many uses: now it became the vehicle of a "mulligan"; anon it would hold our potatoes or coffee. I once happened to refer to it as the *sine qua non,* having regard to its varied uses. The term took [the guide] Bodie's fancy mightily; it became then and thenceforth the "sinkienon"; and I have no doubt it is the sinkienon today, to the perplexity of other travelers under his convoy. Its shape, a portly spheroid supported upon three Falstaffian legs, made the sinkienon something of a problem in packing. By experience we found that it traveled best seated on the top of one of the packs, securely lashed to keep it in place. In this position it resembled some stout captive, or Begum, in a howdah. It was always the last to be lifted up, and the first to be lifted down; and when Jack or Clementine ran amuck our first anxiety was ever for its safety.

Joseph Smeaton Chase, *Yosemite Trails; Camp and Pack-Train in the Yosemite Region of the Sierra Nevada* (New York: Houghton Mifflin Co., 1911)

Manning-Bowman Alcohol Gas Stove advertisment, *Harper's Weekly Advertiser,* November 6, 1909

"Our Worthy Chef," near Calistoga, California, 1898,
University of California, Berkeley, Summer School of
Surveying, from the Oliver Family Photograph Collection

"Meet Mr. Billyan and Mr. Abbott and Mr. Billyan's
stove (one cylinder, but hitting on all cylinders),"
Death Valley Automobile Trip, 1926

"Eat from tin! I could never do that" is a not infrequent exclamation of people who are ignorant of the joys of camp life. It would be hard to find anyone who likes dainty linen and delicate china, at home, better than our campers, but at the same time they think that there is nothing like tin for the woods. It is compact, takes little room, is easily washed and wiped, never breaks, and the fact that one never eats from it at home gives the element of complete change, which is one of the fascinations of camping.

Samuel J. Barrows and Isabel C. Barrows, *The Shaybacks in Camp: Ten Summers under Canvas* (Boston: Houghton Mifflin and Co., 1887)

I believe strongly in the use of cereals in camp. They are compact, good to work on, and offer variety, because they can be cooked in many different ways. Oatmeal, corn meal, rice, and hominy constitute by far the greater part of my provisions. Perhaps I carry my ideas too far for some persons, for once, as I was returning from exploring some glaciers in the northern Rocky Mountains, I overheard one of the men discontentedly reply to someone who asked if we had killed much game. "Oh no; we just lived on mush and glaciers during the whole trip."

"Comfort in Camp," editors of *Harper's Weekly*, October 3, 1896

Longhurst came upon the boards as a flapjack-frier — a role to which he bent his whole intelligence, and with entire success. Scorning such vulgar accomplishment as turning the cake over in mid-air, he slung it boldly up, turning it three times — ostentatiously greasing the pan with a fine centrifugal movement, and catching the flapjack as it fluttered down — and spanked it upon the hot coals with a touch at once graceful and masterly. I failed to enjoy these products, feeling as if I were breakfasting in sacrilege upon works of art.

Clarence King, *Mountaineering in the Sierra Nevada* (Boston: J. R. Osgood and Co., 1872)

"A sample of breakfast," Death Valley Automobile Trip, 1926

"Miss Cathcart, Mother and I cooking breakfast out to Monday Flat. Bully Hill ladies having al fresco breakfast," Shasta County, California, undated, from the Bully Hill Mine Photographs relating to the Lawrence May Family

Everything has the flavor of the wilderness and free life. It is idyllic. And yet, with all our sentimentality, there is nothing feeble about the cooking. The slapjacks are a solid job of work, made to last, and not go to pieces in a person's stomach like a trivial bun: we might record on them, in cuneiform characters, our incipient civilization; and future generations would doubtless turn them up as Acadian bricks.

Charles Dudley Warner, "In the Wilderness," *Atlantic Monthly,* 1878

"Emma annihilating a flapjack,"
Kings River Canyon, California,
1900, from the Joseph N. LeConte
Photograph Collection

[January 30, 1851] ... As for victuals, we have learned to simplify the process of cooking, and perhaps to regard quantity rather than quality. When the campfire is built, a mass of snow, held near it on a wooden fork, soon becomes like a well-filled sponge and furnishes water for coffee and drinking purposes. Also, in making bread, a little snow is put into the mouth of a sack of flour and kneaded carefully until a stiff dough is formed; then lifting it out, it is molded with the hands until of proper consistency for bread. It is then suspended near the fire, on a bough, with several branches cut and sharpened for the purpose. Turning it occasionally, the cake is soon thoroughly baked. Sometimes a slice of bacon is suspended on a wooden fork by the fire and as it fries, the fat is permitted to fall on the bread, thus making it more palatable. It is astonishing how small a culinary outfit is really needed.

General John Bidwell, "Echoes of the Past about California," in *Century Magazine*, 1890

Pioneer settlers of the Sacramento Valley, John and Annie Bidwell were regular tent dwellers. A rancher, politician, philanthropist, and amateur botanist and geologist, John Bidwell led the first wagon train to California in 1841. His beloved wife, Annie, was a suffragist and environmentalist whose friendship and correspondence with John Muir lasted thirty-seven years.

Who has not met with camp-made bread,
Rolled out of putty and weighted with lead?

Snow Bread: After a fall of light, feathery snow, superior corn bread may be made by stirring together 1 quart corn meal, ½ teaspoonful soda, 1 teaspoonful salt, 1 tablespoonful lard. Then in a cool place where snow will not melt, stir into above one quart light snow. Bake about forty minutes in rather hot oven. Snow, for some unknown reason, has the same effect on corn bread as eggs have, two tablespoonfuls of snow equaling one egg. It can also be used in making batter for pancakes, the batter being made rather thick, and the snow mixed with each cake just before putting in the pan.

Horace Kephart, *The Book of Camping and Woodcraft* (New York: Outing Publishing Co., 1906)

We made good progress, and about noon rested and had a piece of bread each. Bob had the remainder in a flour sack, and after walking a short distance, we again stopped to rest on a log, as we had lost the trail. Underneath and all around was water, black and brackish, as the ground here was swampy. Well, Bob dropped his sack and bread into this concern. We fished it out and emptied the bread and wrung the water out of the sack, replaced the bread and were soon on the road. In about two hours more, we made our camping ground, and lighting a fire, we split our wet bread and toasted it for supper. We ate it but would have much preferred something else.

James Wilson, "A Trip in the Cascade Mountains," 1883, manuscript

Club Bread: Cut a club two feet long and three inches thick at the broadest end; peel or shave off the bark smoothly, and sharpen the smaller end neatly. Then stick the sharpened end in the ground near the fire, leaning the broad end toward a bed of live coals, where it will get screeching hot. While it is heating, mix rather more than a half pint of best Minnesota flour with enough warm water to make a dough. Add a half teaspoonful of salt, and a teaspoonful of sugar, and mould and pull the dough until it becomes lively. Now, work it into a ribbon two inches wide and half an inch thick, wind the ribbon spirally around the broad end of the club, stick the latter in front of the fire so that the bread will bake evenly and quickly to a light brown, and turn frequently until done, which will be in about thirty minutes. When done, take it from the fire, stand the club firmly upright, and pick the bread off in pieces as you want it to eat. It will keep hot a long time, and one soon becomes fond of it.

"Nessmuk," *Woodcraft* (New York: Forest and Stream Publishing Co., 1884)

"Making pull biscuit," Kings River Canyon, California, 1900, Joseph N. LeConte Photograph Collection

Ash Cakes: Mix up a pint of corn meal with water and a pinch of salt into a stiff dough, make into cakes, and set them on a clean, hot stone close to the coals of a hot fire. When the outside of the cakes has hardened a little, cover them completely in hot ashes. In fifteen to twenty-five minutes rake them out, brush off the ashes, and devour quickly.

"Seneca," *Canoe and Camp Cookery: A Practical Cook Book* (New York: Forest and Stream Publishing Co., 1885)

Father baked the bread over the fire, then with two sticks balanced nicely the two cakes on each side of the fire. They gave him a great deal of trouble though, one was always falling down in the sand just as he was picking up and wiping and balancing the other.

Diary entry, Caroline Eaton LeConte, Yosemite, June 1878, LeConte Family Papers

In warm weather, one's first few days in the open air will bring an inordinate thirst, which is not caused by the stomach's demand for water, but by a fever of the palate. This may be relieved somewhat by chewing a green leaf, or by carrying a smooth, non-absorbent pebble in the mouth; but a much better thirst-quencher is a bit of raw onion carried in the mouth. One can go a long time without drinking if he has an onion with him; this also prevents one's lips from cracking in alkali dust.

Horace Kephart, *The Book of Camping and Woodcraft* (New York: Outing Publishing Co., 1906)

1. If knives become rusty, rub them with a fresh-cut potato dipped in ashes.
2. Gunpowder dissolved in water is a good emetic.
3. If you make tea do not throw out the "grounds" after each drawing. In warm weather, ordinary lake or river water will taste very refreshing if poured into the pot where tea grounds have been left, and allowed to stand for a few minutes.
4. Boil a handful of grass in a new iron pot, then scrub it inside with soap and sand, fill it with clean water, and let this boil half an hour. It is then ready to use for cooking.

"Seneca," *Canoe and Camp Cookery: A Practical Cook Book* (New York: Forest and Stream Publishing Co., 1885)

"Cooking trout on rocks, Kings River Canyon,"
1929, Joseph N. LeConte Photograph Collection

Huckleberries were plentiful and we gathered about four or five gallons and I made pie. I first put the berries on the fire in the dutch oven, and boiled them a little, then I poured the water off and mashed them up some, then took some of the juice and made paste with it, then put the berries in between two pastes and baked in the oven. They tasted very tough and tart, but we praised them and considered them splendid.

James Wilson, "A Trip in the Cascade Mountains," 1883, manuscript

Some days, mounting his pony, he would ride up the stream, picking flowers, gathering wild raspberries, or whatever his fancy led him to do. One day he found a bed of mint, near the foot of a snow bank, and, breaking off a large piece of the icy snow, he brought it into camp in a large burlap sack that he had underneath his saddle, and when the rest of the party came in at evening he had a mint julep ready for us.

Joseph A. Thatcher, *A Colorado Outing* (Denver, Colo.: Smith-Brooks, 1905)

Thatcher is referring to one of four campers on the outing, Jack Rolfson, "a South Carolinian, a college man, a graduate at the law school of his state, a lover of books, a musical enthusiast, and a dreamer."

David Brower also had a recipe for mountaintop mint juleps. He would muddle pennyroyal-mint leaves over the embossed Sierra Club logo at the bottom of his ever-present tin cup, adding snow and flask whiskey to taste.

From Tenaya Camp we straggled to Soda Springs. . . . There we found camp pitched in a pine grove by the riverside, Tie Sing already grinning over his sheet iron stove. . . . For most of us this was a first view of the Geological Survey's famous Chinese cook, whose clever manipulation of his primitive outfit was to afford us so much satisfaction during the following fortnight. To me Tie Sing had assumed apocryphal proportions. The extraordinary recitals of his astonishing culinary exploits had been more than I could quite believe. But I believe them all now, and more. I shall not forget that dinner;—soup, trout, chops, fried

"Tie Sing—Wizard"; Edward S. Curtis, photographer; from Robert Sterling Yard's "The John Muir Trail: A Brief Account of the [Stephen] Mather Mountain Party's Outing of 1916," manuscript, in the Francis P. Farquhar Pictorial Collection

potatoes, string beans, fresh bread, hot apple pie, cheese and coffee. It was the first of many equally elaborate, and equally appreciated. Nor shall I forget our first night. The moon rising full over Dana and Gibbs touched with glory the twisted horns of Unicorn Peak, and no doubt grinned as she peered through the pines at eight men lying flat on their stomachs blowing lusty blasts into sleeping bags.

Robert Sterling Yard, "The John Muir Trail: A Brief Account of the Mather Mountain Party's Outing of 1916," 1918, Francis P. Farquhar Photograph Collection

Stephen Mather organized a series of Yosemite expeditions in his campaign to win support for the establishment of the National Park Service. Augmented by cooks and aides, the groups traveled in rustic splendor, though the ever exuberant Mather liked to awaken his colleagues by letting the air out of their air-mattresses. Newspaperman Yard kept a journal of the second trip, which was later illustrated with photographs of the trip taken by Edward Curtis.

Early on Monday morning, May 22d, it would have been amusing to have stood in front of the hotel to witness the novel excitement of packing provisions, furniture, &c., for our strange journey among the mountains. Determined not to fall into the error of some, who have taken the trip without paying proper attention to the commissariat department, we loaded our pack mule with a good supply of stuffs for culinary use. Our bill of fare consisted of preserved chickens and oysters, pork and beans, soda biscuit, potatoes, preserved fruits, and some medicinal antidotes against the poisonous bite of rattlesnakes, which abound in the Valley. During the journey, our guns added to the store fine venison, grouse, mountain quail, grizzly bear; and from the stream we caught a few trout. Having completed the outfit, we mounted our steeds, and with high hopes, left the borders of civilization.

James Denman, "The Sublime and the Beautiful of California," in the *San Francisco Evening Bulletin*, June 27, 1857

"The Dining Room," Mt. Shasta, July 1888,
from the Frank B. Rodolph Photograph Collection

September 3, 1877, North Fork, Russian River. As we had plenty of time, it was determined to get up a meal that would do justice to such epicures as we were. Three of the boys were appointed cooks. Our bill of fare included Broiled Venison, Mashed Potatoes, Baked ditto, Pork Stew, Quail on Toast, Pancakes, Fresh Bread, Biscuits, and black coffee. We very appropriately named this stopping place *Square Meal Camp*. Whilst we were eating, the stage passed us and we gave them a roared cheer. And so we lived: forgetting everything in the animal spirit that animated us.

Diary entry, Frank B. Rodolph, manuscript

The "outfit" consisted of sixteen souls, all much emaciated by a steady diet of hoecakes, fried ham, and canned vegetables. The poor creatures made a desperate effort to seem contented with their lot, and even strove to crack some ghastly jokes on the subject, but the ravenous, not to say wolfish, manner in which they gazed at the first-class civilized lunch, produced and devoured by this writer's party, would have softened the hardest heart.

During our visit, the usual regular morning quarrel as to whose turn it was to cut firewood for the next meal took place. This singular daily observance of the campers' species was conducted with great vim and bitterness, and lasted over two hours.

It is amid the modern camping party that cookery of the cookbook variety has full sweep in the terrible work of destruction. There is always, we are naively assured by the fair promoters of such schemes, a certain Miss Smith, or Jones, who is celebrated for her muffins, or who is sure of a lofty niche in the temple of fame in consequence of some particularly gorgeous brand of sponge-cake brewed by her. In fact, all the young females implicated in these nefarious plots against the comfort and well-being of the commonwealth have some particular dish they are supposed to manufacture with peculiar skill. The result is that the mortality of these mutual misery associations is something enormous, and which is, doubtless, the reason they are so popular with the coroners of the cow counties. At the before-mentioned camp, for illustration, we met a friend who, only two short months ago, was one of the most promising young lawyers of Sacramento. As we gazed upon the cadaverous figure, broken down by a severe course of fried beefsteak and burnt coffee, we could scarcely recognize our stalwart young jurist of yesterday. Taking our arm, with feeble steps he led us to a retired spot in the grove. There, in broken accents, he explained that his fiancée was one of his party, and that she had a mania for making biscuits with saleratus. Producing what appeared to be a circular piece of yellow adamant from his pocket, he exhibited a sample. Hard tack was as a cream-puff compared to it. "I have been living on this sort of thing for twenty-one days," said the victim. "Another week will finish me. Tell them that I feel resigned, and have my name carved on one of these biscuits for a headstone," and he sobbed con-vulsively as he confided to us his will and a few last messages to his friends. It was with a heavy heart that we drove off, and left the poor wretch to his fate.

"Derrick Dodd" (pseudonym of Frank Harrison Gassaway), *Summer Saunterings* (San Francisco: Francis, Valentine & Co., 1882)

W hat adjective shall we find to do justice to that . . . sustaining viand, [bacon]? . . . It strengthens the arm while it satisfies the palate. Crisp, juicy, savory; delicately salt as the breeze that blows from the sea; faintly pungent as the blue smoke of incense wafted from a clean wood fire; aromatic, appetizing, nourishing, a stimulant to the hunger that appeases . . . brought by the art of man's device to a perfec-tion surpassing nature. All problems of wood-land cookery are best solved by the baconian method.

Elizabeth Keith Pond, Mountain Journal III, August 1924, Keith-McHenry-Pond Papers

"Stopped for lunch in a meadow, on Sunrise Trail from Yosemite Valley to Tuolumne Meadows," January 14, 1914. Elizabeth Keith Pond Mountain Journals, Keith-McHenry-Pond Family Papers

You have never had a soda fountain delicacy that quite hit the spot as does snow sherbet after you've climbed in the sun till you feel like a toasted cracker. The easiest way to make it is by mixing snow and jam in a cup or right in a little hollow in the snowbank. Strawberry and apricot jam both do very well.

A superior variety is made with fresh lemon juice and sugar; orange juice is also excellent.

Louise Hildebrand and Joel H. Hildebrand, *Camp Catering* (Brattleboro, Vt.: Stephen Daye Press, 1938)

Louise Hildebrand coauthored a camp cookbook with her father, Joel, a chemistry professor at the University of California and president of the Sierra Club.

June 28th [1934] . . . Supper, after such a day [of climbing,] was something to be appreciated. We had been cooking beans since the day before yesterday (necessary at 10,500') and they were done. So with a cup of flour, salt, baking powder, and water I mixed up more batter, to which was added the left-over combination oatmeal-cornmeal mush of breakfast time; and the resultant was fried in deep bacon fat on our granite range, three panfuls at a time. We stopped at 13, and then, adding sugar syrup and washing down with cocoa, we had a tasty supper, difficult as it may be to believe.

Diary entry, David Ross Brower, David Ross Brower Papers

"An alpine camp at 10,000 ft. elevation with equipment for attempting the unclimbed peaks near the Sawtooth Ridge, July 26, 1934," from the Richard M. Leonard Photograph Collection of Rock Climbing Techniques

Lawyer and mountaineer Dick Leonard pioneered the use of nylon rope and expansion anchors to refine rock climbing techniques, and worked tirelessly in environmental litigation. The canvas "tree pockets" hanging at the top of the photograph were common and convenient camp furnishings.

February 29, 1936, fourth attempt of Mt. Lyell by Bestor Robinson, Lewis Clark, Boynton ("Bunco") Kaiser, Einar Nilsson, and David Brower — By the time sleeping bags, knapsacks, and men had been piled inside the two tiny tents, the congestion was quite cozy. Sole evidence of the wind outside was the powder that sifted through every available aperture, to the syncopated accompaniment of flapping tent fabric. Having snow inside was an advantage, since it was no longer necessary to reach outside to get it for melting over our Primus stoves. Bestor, Lewis, and Bunco prepared the soup on their stove [in their tent]. Einar and I improvised an entrée of chocolate, cheese, and oatmeal [in our tent]. With everything ready, dinner was served: a momentary lull in the gale was awaited, tent flaps were unzipped, victuals passed frantically so that we could rezip before the next snow-laden gust.

David Ross Brower, "Beyond the Skiways," in the *Sierra Club Bulletin*, vol. 23, no. 2, April 1938

Dinner is quite a function. It is there, perhaps, that you catch most fully the charm, the picturesqueness, and the jollity of the outing. Behind the long table stand eight girls dressed in the brightest and best their dunnage-bags can offer — shirt-waists fresh from the river, skirts a shade longer and cleaner than the well-worn regimentals, and caps, aprons, and kerchiefs of gaudy bandanas. Each girl has charge of a kettle and a spoon, and for an hour or more hungry people file past the table for a second, third, even a fourth, helping — soup, fresh meat, potatoes, bread and butter, rice, tomatoes, pudding, gingerbread, tea and coffee *à la* tin cow, surely a meal fit for the gods.

Marion Randall, "Some Aspects of a Sierra Club Outing," in the *Sierra Club Bulletin*, vol. 5, no. 3, January 1905

"Serving dinner," Kern River and Mt. Whitney High Trip, 1903; Joseph N. LeConte; Sierra Club Photograph Albums

Photograph by Orland Bartholomew from Sierra Nevada Photographs, 1928

Memorialized in a biography entitled *High Odyssey,* Orland "Bart" Bartholomew in 1929 made a three-month, three-hundred-mile solo midwinter trek, skiing the Sierra crest from south of Mt. Whitney to Yosemite National Park, making the first winter ascent of Mt. Whitney (the highest peak in the lower forty-eight states) and traveling without the amenities of a sleeping bag or tent.

FIVE

Snags and Hitches

Mosquitoes, scorpions, critter-commandeered food supplies, heat and chill, lost trails, sudden downpours, and similar botherments have plagued outdoor living since long before it was pursued for sport and amusement. But sometimes, it appears that the wetter the blankets and the harder the trail, the clearer the memories and the better the story. And at any rate, the tribulations didn't keep the campers home.

Earlier in the season, before we had realized that wind must be considered in choosing a campground in that part of New Mexico, thinking of the view, we had camped on the edge of a high sandstone ledge, commanding a glorious expanse of star-filled sky at night, and overlooking the dry wash of the Agua Nigra Chiquita with its juniper and nut pine–dotted basin. Through this, long freight trains passed on their way between Kansas City and El Paso, and at midnight the overland sleeper with its lighted coaches thundered by.

Our tent was pitched between a juniper and a fragrant piñon pine near the edge of the cliff and our floor was strewn with pine needles and aromatic chunks of pitch that intensified the delicious piney odors coming from the low, glistening trees around us. . . . After a warm, quiet day, at sunset gathering clouds, wind, thunder, and lightning made us run an extra rope under the peak of the tent, tighten the guy ropes, lay heavy stones along the bottom to reinforce the pins, and stand the grips on stones inside the tent . . . With these preparations we retired to the tent and tied the flaps together. We were none too soon. Roaring through the trees came a sand-filled gale that struck the back of the tent with such force that it ripped it open halfway to the ground. Springing up, the Naturalist [husband Vernon Bailey] seized the

torn sides and, twisting them together, held them in a grip of iron while I seized the whipping tent flaps and held onto them till the gale fought itself out and big drops of rain began to fall. A heavy downpour followed and as we held the tent together in the darkness we cheered ourselves by telling the Tenderfoot tales of cloudbursts and floods on the Pecos, Colorado, Brazos, and Rio Grande, which "get up" and sweep everything before them, from thousands of helpless sheep to campers on their banks.

Florence Merriam Bailey, "By the Light of the Campfire," 1903, Florence Merriam Bailey Papers

The swollen river was a tremendous thing to be near, because you could hear the boulders going down the river at night. Night was when the high water came—after the sun had melted the snow in the daytime. The high water would reach the Kings River Canyon a little after midnight and you could hear these great boulders —huge things!—come bumping down the middle of the river. It would shake and jar the ground. By golly that was something!

Hal Roth, Interview with William E. Colby, February 27, 1961, manuscript

—A HARD BLOW—

"A Hard Blow," by Charles [Carlos] J. Hittell, 1881, from the Honeyman Collection of Early Californian and Western American Pictorial Material

As a child, Charles Hittell accompanied his father, Theodore, and his uncle John, both noted California historians, on family camping trips. When he was twenty-three, Charles traveled to Paris with his friend William Keith to study art, and while there adopted the name Carlos and dressed flamboyantly in spurs and a ten-gallon cowboy hat that had been given to him by Buffalo Bill.

Every summer the dells and openings of the Coast Range are merry with the voices of those who, tired of luxury and of the monotony of a quiet life, abandon their comfortable homes for the fascinations of savagism. The Californian camper for his sins is placed beneath a broiling sun so hot as to melt bones and evaporate brain; streams come panting from the hills bereft of every refreshing quality save wetness, and the noiseless breeze is stifling as from an oven; lizards creep over the blistering stones, and the heated sands in treading on them feel to the feet like the newly emptied ashes of a furnace; glistening snakes trail through the silvery incandescent grass, and bloodless winged insects dance through the short day of their existence. Every cool shade is preempted by mosquitoes, and every inviting nook entertains with poison oak. Before the tired hunter who with blistered feet and lacerated limbs climbs the craggy hills, the game flees yet weary miles away, and the patient fisherman sits by the stream all day without a nibble. Add to these evils rats and reptiles as bed-fellows, the burnings of indigestion arising

from the poorly cooked meats, and the little bickerings and disagreements inseparable from all but the most sensible or amiable of associates.

Hubert Howe Bancroft, *Literary Industries: A Memoir* (San Francisco: History Co., 1891)

San Francisco publisher and historian Hubert Howe Bancroft developed a passion for collecting and compiled from his collected materials a prodigious thirty-nine-volume history of the West. Literary Industries, *the thirty-ninth volume, is largely autobiographical, allowing Bancroft to air his views and opinions on myriad topics. His vast collection of books, manuscripts, ephemera, and photographs became* The Bancroft Library *at the University of California, Berkeley, in 1905.*

Before it was daylight the sky was overcast, for the sea-fog had come in on the wings of the morn — an arrangement that is always agreeable to me, since it allows of breakfast being cooked without enduring a superfluous blast of sun. I confess I find the manufacture of flapjacks over a smoky fire, with a fervent sun castigating me from above, an exercise that puts too much strain upon the early morning temper.

Joseph Smeaton Chase, *California Coast Trails; a Horseback Ride from Mexico to Oregon* (Boston, New York: Houghton Mifflin Co., 1913)

"Ranger's Camp. A Cold Morning," Kings River Camp, 1929, from the Joseph N. LeConte Photograph Collection

The Granite Basin camp, at an altitude of 10,400 feet, was a strange beautiful place, with gray rock scenery that looked like that of the moon. There was a moon, too, shedding a weird loveliness down upon our camp-fire gathering. And that night a heavy frost. In the morning the few long-haired women had to shatter the ice from their rigid locks while the bobbed-hair sisterhood was jauntily off for hot coffee.

Bertha Clark Pope, "The High Trip of 1925," in the *Sierra Club Bulletin*, vol. 12, no. 3, 1926

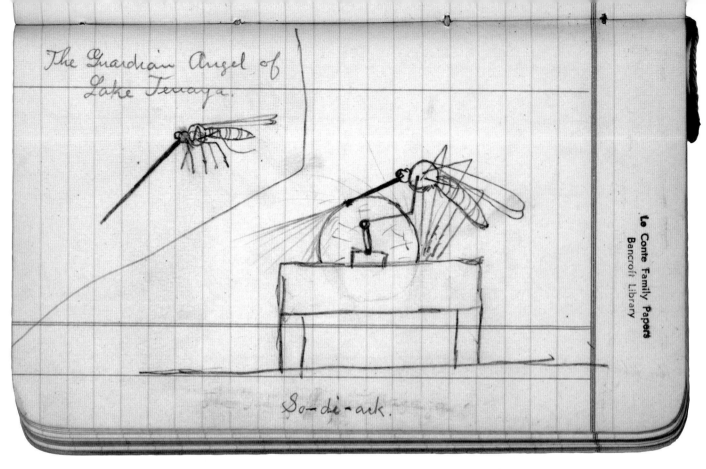

The Guardian Angel of
Lake Tenaya.

So-di-ack.

"The Guardian Angel of
Lake Tenaya, So-di-ack,"
diary entry by Joseph N.
LeConte, July 1893,
from the LeConte
Family Papers

We were driven from Stockton by the mosquitoes, and moved on to Sacramento, intending to reach the Putah Creek Mountains through Yolo County. The trip from Sacramento to Woodland was one of much difficulty on account of a tule swamp, through a portion of which we were obliged to drive. After a considerable balky mule, and a number of mishaps, we reached Woodland, the thriving county town of Yolo. We camped on the railroad station grounds near the village, under a large live oak tree. I cannot say how many ants there were under that tree, but think it might be put at 5,000,000. The body of the tree was alive with them. All the other trees about us entertained the same population.

Dio Lewis, M.D., *Gypsies, or Why We Went Gypsying in the Sierras* (Boston: Eastern Book Co., 1881)

For mosquitoes and other poisonous insects: Three ounces of pine tar, two ounces castor oil, one ounce pennyroyal oil. Simmer all together over a slow fire, and bottle for use. One ounce has lasted me six weeks in the woods. Rub it in thoroughly and liberally at first, and after you have established a good glaze, a little replenishing from day to day will be sufficient. And don't fool with soap and towels where insects are plenty. A good safe coat of this varnish grows better the longer it is kept on — and it is cleanly and wholesome . . . I found the mixture gave one's face the ruddy tanned look supposed to be indicative of health and hard muscle.

"Nessmuk," *Woodcraft* (New York: Forest and Stream Publishing Co., 1884)

Upon returning to camp I found the first rattlesnake of the season had arrived and was enjoying my blankets in the tent. He seemed firm but calm, as if open to any reasonable offer. While I sought a tripod he vanished. In the night I felt something creeping over my chest under the blankets, and with panic remembered my visitor, who might have come to claim a share of the accommodation. I made a really brilliant jump, struck a match, and met the reproachful gaze of a large, stout, comatose lizard that was searching affectionately for the nice warm bedfellow who had suddenly turned unkind.

J. Smeaton Chase, *California Desert Trails* (Boston and New York: Houghton Mifflin Co., 1919)

After an hour or more of rough scrambling through brush and over talus, we willingly confessed we had had enough experience for one day, and were ready to stop at the first comfortable camping place. Here a mild discussion arose between the two members of our party as to what constituted a good sleeping spot, when we must rest for the night with neither blankets nor down sleeping bags for a covering. Mr. Price declared himself in favor of a bed of leaves, with a great fire on either side, and I advocated the advantages of a sand bank, where the flame could not reach us unknowingly. But nature did not seem to heed my decision, for we traveled on and on, and found no sleeping place such as I desired. Finally an inviting spot under the trees near the river was selected, and tossing off our knapsacks with great satisfaction, we were soon enjoying a supper of corn-meal mush, dried apricots, and beef bouillon. After finishing our meal, I left Mr. Price to gather wood while I repaired to the river to wash our few cooking utensils. It was not long before I saw my husband in great distress, gesticulating wildly, and rushing toward the stream in strangest fashion, motioning me to leave the spot where I stood spellbound. For a moment I could not think at all; then a confusion of emotions passed through my mind, and finally I thought of snakes. The stories of rattlers and their abundance in the cañon had not been a pleasant prospect from the beginning; and now, on our first night, we had been attacked, and Mr. Price probably bitten. In great anxiety I awaited his approach, and, finally, above the roar of the water, I made out that the cause of all my fears, and Mr. Price's gesticulations, was nothing more dangerous than wasps. Sleep, we knew, in the vicinity of a disturbed wasps' nest, with a fire to keep the insects stirring, was next to impossible; so, quickly gathering our belongings, in the darkness we made our way along the stream in quest of a new sleeping ground. It was no pleasure at that late hour to drag our weary limbs over jagged rocks that often tripped our careless feet, or to slip every now and then, in spite of ourselves, into little pools of cold water; but fortunately, we had not far to travel, and this time it was a sand bank we found. An ideal spot it was, sheltered on three sides by huge boulders that acted as reflectors for the heat of the fire, and having ready, within reach, wood of all shapes and sizes, tossed there by spring torrents. Sleeping without blankets was a novel experience, but not as uncomfortable as would be expected. With leggings for a pillow, we managed to sleep the greater part of the night, rousing ourselves at long intervals to replenish our fire.

Jennie Ellsworth Price, "A Woman's Trip through the Tuolumne Cañon," in the *Sierra Club Bulletin,* vol. 2, no. 3, January 1898

John Muir told Jennie Price after her trip that she was the first American woman to have made it through the canyon.

"Russian River Recreation, May 1868," by Theodore H. Hittell, from the Hittell Family Papers

About 2 p.m., as we were looking out for a camping-ground, a thunderstorm again burst upon us. We hurried on, searching among the huge boulders (probably glacial boulders), to find a place of shelter for our provisions and ourselves. At last we found a huge boulder which overhung on one side, leaning against a large tree. The roaring of the coming storm grows louder and louder, the pattering of rain already commences. "Quick! quick!!" In a few seconds the pack was unsaddled, and provisions thrown under shelter. Then rolls of blankets quickly thrown after them; then the horses unsaddled and tied; then, at last, we ourselves, though already wet, crowded under. It was an interesting and somewhat amusing sight. All our provisions and blanket rolls and eleven men packed away, actually piled upon one another, under a rock which did not project more than two and a half feet. I wish I could draw a picture of

the scene; the huge rock with its dark recess; the living, squirming mass, piled confusedly beneath; the magnificent forest of grand trees; the black clouds; the constant gleams of lightning, revealing the scarcely visible faces; the peals of thunder, and the floods of rain, pouring from the rock on the projecting feet and knees of those whose legs were inconveniently long, or even on the heads and backs of some who were less favored in position.

Joseph LeConte, *A Journal of Ramblings through the High Sierras of California by the "University Excursion Party"* (San Francisco: Francis & Valentine, 1875)

In 1870, Joseph LeConte (the senior), professor of geology at the University of California and trained as a medical doctor, was invited to accompany nine recent university graduates on an adventure of five weeks, from the Bay Area across the San Joaquin Valley to Yosemite, over the Sierra summit to Mono Lake, then north to Lake Tahoe and down the slope for home. His "jotted, wayside notes" became the first of many LeConte family camp diaries. He continued to camp with family and friends until his death in a tent in Yosemite over the 1901 Fourth of July week-end. His friend John Muir, first met on the 1870 trip, said of his death, "These mountain mansions are decent, delightful, even divine places to die when compared with the doleful chambers of civilization."

"Is the axe sharp?" inquired my companion in camping as I busied myself cutting a supply of wood.

"No, not especially so," I replied.

Probably the man in question, not being of the cooperative kind, would not have taken the trouble to wield the axe even if it had been in perfect condition. Anyway, the dullness of the only available one served as a sufficient alibi for letting someone else do all the woodcutting during the entire trip.

Norman Clyde, "Cooperation in Camping," undated, from the Norman Clyde Papers

Slept badly last night. Those confounded sand flies, how they everlastingly go for a fellow; but a person can hardly blame them, they get a chance at a fellow so seldom that they want to make up for lost time.

We had old bacon sacks with us, and we took off our shoes and pulled the sacks up around our legs and tried to sleep. Sometime during the night, I was roused by a yell that I thought must be a war whoop, and sprang up expecting to see all the Indians in the country looking for a lock of my hair. Instead I found Bob on fire. The sack he wrapped his legs in had come in contact with a fallen ember, and being full of bacon grease, caught fire and the poor fellow's toes were burned almost to a cinder. We smothered the fire as soon as possible. I then took out the linseed oil, poured it on his feet and then took some salt and spread it on top of the oil. It pained him very much of course, but it was the best that could be done under the circumstances.

James Wilson, "A Trip in the Cascade Mountains," 1883, manuscript

"Overflow crowd of campers in Stoneman Meadow," circa 1915, from "Environmental Effects of Tourism at Yosemite National Park," manuscript

"Jim and Joe," Mt. Brewer and Mt. Whitney, California, 1895;
Joseph N. LeConte; from the Sierra Club Photograph Albums

When he was twenty-five, "Little Joe" LeConte posed for the camera with his pal Jim.

SIX

Campmates

Camping begets camaraderie—communal destinations, tents, and chores make for fast friendships, forged over smoky campfires. The ability of the out-of-doors to cement these bonds contributes to the success and popularity of enduring group camps—YMCA, Scout, church, school, city, or environmental organization. Camping, unsurprisingly, fosters tolerance and cooperation. The shared experiences of being lost, trying to cook over an open fire, reaching the pinnacle, ineffable silliness, and the absence of society's stringencies lead campers to let their hat-hair down and await the next opportunity to pitch the tents.

Bloomers made of brown or blue denim, two and one-half yards to the leg, plaited at the waist and gathered below the knee into a four or five inch cuff, to hold the bloomers within the boot. I condemn khaki, it is harsh and graceless and not serviceable; soils too easily. The great drawback to bloomers generally is their scantiness and poor fit; bloomers are models of grace and comfort when made of the right material by the right party — they are cool and clean and warm; never flop on the saddle or hang in the brush; never trip your toe with an inner hem when you carry a loaded gun — they are also immune from the attacks of bugs and spiders. I proclaim that those women who refuse to wear bloomers on an outing are suffering from mock modesty.

Vernille DeWitt Warr, "A Woman in the Wilds," in *Western Field*, January 1912

After a summer spent on Mt. Tallac, Mt. Zora, and Freels Peak, in the Lake Tahoe area, this California suffragist, dramatic reader, and self-described love psychologist wrote of camping at eleven thousand feet and admonished other women to be "super-up-to-date twentieth century women" and take to the hills.

Even in 1921 the camp [in Yosemite] was full of people. Camping became the thing to do in the summer. It was the style and that is why my mother wanted to go camping. Both my mother and grandmother had the latest camping clothes with their divided skirts. My father had riding pants that fitted into leather putties.

Erwin Strohmaier, "California History: Early Vacations," Erwin Strohmaier Family Papers

Nowhere on earth, I think, does one so relish food and drink as around the campfire. And of all places on earth for solid comfort in camp there is none like California. The pure, dry, mountain air is always so healthful and invigorating, and the nice, dry ground is worth all the spring mattresses in Christendom for a bed. And then it never rains in California during the spring, summer, and autumn months. Given a shot-gun, a rifle, fishing-tackle, blankets to sleep in, a frying-pan, coffee-pot and cups, a little flour, salt, pepper, and a few sundries, and a bunch of matches, and, with two or three jolly companions — it is none the worse if the party is half made up of ladies, so that they are possessed of sense and know how to rough it and enjoy it — your "outfit" is complete.

Albert S. Evans, *A la California: Sketches of Life in the Golden State* (San Francisco: A. L. Bancroft, 1873)

Maybel I. Davis, Estelle
Sweet, Bertha Sweet, and
Mabel Sweet, on a trip to
Yosemite with Adolph Sweet
and Theodore Solomons, 1896;
Theodore Solomons, photo-
grapher; Francis P. Farquhar
Photograph Collection

June 16 Tuesday, [1896]. Spent the morning looking for feed for the horses. Then climbed mountain. Got back at 4 p.m. when the girls took a dip in the lake in a spot where the ice had melted. They took turns. Each one with a rope tied around her would jump in and be pulled out by the other 3. We were not allowed on that side of the mountain but heard the yelling miles away.

June 21, Sunday. Up before daylight as could not sleep. Thermometer showed 10 degrees above zero. . . . During night the girls' bedding, already burned in several places, caught fire and was blazing away and some large holes were burned in the canvas cover and blankets, one of Bertha's leggings was burned up. I threw several buckets of water on their bedding, putting out the fire, but not even waking them. By pooling their blankets and sleeping together the 4 girls slept fairly warm. Solomons had a special eiderdown sleeping bag for himself and always slept comfortably. I had a half blanket and did not sleep at all. If you don't believe it — try sleeping in the snow at an altitude of 8,000 to 10,000 feet and try to keep covered with a half blanket. I made up for it in the daytime for I fell fast asleep every time we stopped and had to be waked up to get on my feet again. . . . After a sketchy breakfast started out again groaning under our packs. Struck more swampy land thick with quaking aspen on canyon bottom and had to climb several times up and down the granite chimneys in order to travel. Solomons in the lead and yours truly bringing up the rear. In climbing down a particularly dangerous chimney, I had to take a jump to a small landing below. I jumped all right, but my pack caught between the narrow walls of the chimney, leaving me dangling several hundred feet from the bottom of the cliff. How long I hung there fearful of making any abrupt move I don't know. But I wondered at first if they would miss me and come back to my rescue. I must have been there a long time when suddenly I

commenced to slip loose and landed safely on the only safe spot. I hurried to catch up with the party expecting to get a lot of sympathy, but instead was lectured for delaying the party.

Adolph D. Sweet, "Down a Glacier a Mile a Minute," in *Tulare County Historical Society Bulletin* No. 7, March 1951, Visalia, California

Adolph Sweet's diary of his camping trip into the Grand Canyon of the Tuolumne River with Theodore Solomons as guide and four University of California students — Maybel I. Davis and his sisters Estelle, Bertha, and Mabel Sweet — was published forty-five years later in this historical society bulletin. The trip was first described in the San Francisco Chronicle *on August 25, 1896. Though not seeming to share in the carefree fun with the others during the trip, and complaining of having to sleep in swarms of ants and forever chase the horses, Sweet concludes his diary, "When I got on the scales, I found I had gained weight and never before or since have I ever weighed as much or felt so good." The high point of the trip for the women was a "wildly glorious" slide "a mile down Lyell Glacier in a minute," sitting down, each holding on to the girl in front, tobogganing back to the campsite.*

"A desperate looking crowd — except the faces," Sequoia, California, 1902; Myrtle Rossiter Saunders, San Francisco Bay Area Scenes

Claire Tappaan, "Little Joe" LeConte, Bob Price, and William Colby, Sierra Club High Trip, Kings and San Joaquin Rivers, 1925, from Sierra Club Portrait Miscellany

"Four men at bar in tent, Bohemian Grove," Sonoma County, California, before 1918, from the Oliver Family Photograph Collection

The exclusive men-only Bohemian Club was founded by five *San Francisco Examiner* journalists in 1872. Since then the 2700-acre grove near the Russian River has been the site of annual retreats of the wealthy and powerful where camping among the redwoods is hardly rustic.

At Lunch. Hazel Green

"At lunch, Hazel Green," June 1888;
John F. Young, Views in Yosemite Valley

"Camp, Elk River Valley," undated;
Thomas D. Bowman, photographer;
Dane Coolidge Photograph Collection

Car camping by the Mokelumne (?)
River, undated

"The Solid Six; The Bandana Brigade,"
Marion Randall Parsons at far right,
Kings River Canyon, 1906, from the
Joseph N. LeConte Photograph Collection

"Café Moraine," Kern River Canyon
to Mt. Whitney High Trip, 1916;
S. Van Hagen, "The Three Musketeers:
Their Pictures!," Sierra Club Photograph Albums

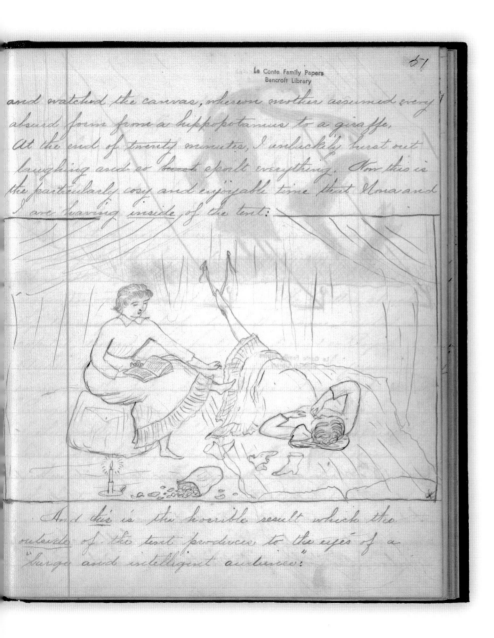

and watched the canvas, whereon mother assumed every absurd form from a hippopotamus to a giraffe. At the end of twenty minutes, I unluckily burst out laughing and so spoilt everything. Now this is the particularly cosy and enjoyable time that Nona and I are having inside of the tent:

And this is the horrible result which the outside of the tent produces to the eyes of a "large and intelligent audience:"

Early in the evening Nona and I retired to explore Nona's valise. We found a great package of delicious sugar-plums, and "Adam Bede," by George Eliot. As neither Nona nor I had ever read "Adam Bede" we sat down and began right away, munching sugar-plums the while, and feeling as comfortable and pleasant as possible. Now there is one thing dreadful about having a candle in the tent: it always makes what I call "charcoal sketches." And if you are not very careful to put the candle on the side *from* the camp-fire, those sitting around the latter may be entertained in a way very diverting to themselves, but rather disagreeable for you. Once, when Mother was giving Joe a bath in the tent, I sat outside for twenty minutes and watched the canvas, whereon Mother assumed every absurd form from a hippopotamus to a giraffe. At the end of twenty minutes, I unluckily burst out laughing and so spoilt everything. Now this [left] is the particularly cozy and enjoyable time that Nona and I are having inside of the tent.

And *this* is the horrible result which the *outside* of the tent produces to the eyes of a "large and intelligent audience":

Diary entry, Caroline Eaton LeConte, Yosemite, June 1878, from the LeConte Family Papers

Le Conte Family Papers
Bancroft Library

June 18th Nona and I were too lazy to get up so as to go to Mirror Lake. When you consider Mirror Lake in bed it wears a very different aspect from Mirror Lake considered at mid-day. It doesn't seem half so charming somehow. The Woolsey girls, Mr. Butters, and the students

Bill and John Pond with Frisky the squirrel, Silver Lake, Plumas County, California, July 12, 1926; Elizabeth Keith Pond Mountain Journals, Keith-McHenry-Pond Family Papers

The *Burlingame Advance-Star* reported on October 7, 1931, that Frisky II, the Pond family's pet squirrel, had safely traversed two hundred miles across California to return to the Pond family home, after having been left in the Sierra the previous June.

It sounds rather alarming at first — to camp for a month with a party of one hundred and fifty persons, strangers for the greater part, gathered from all quarters of California and from distant points throughout the world, representatives of every profession, every science, every art, who have only one common bond, the love of nature. They are very queer-looking people too, some of them. They bear a few hallmarks of civilization, it is true; they take off their hats when they speak to you, and smoke pipes and cigarettes; they possess tooth-brushes and mirrors and back-combs — but you never heard of anything like them in song or story nor saw them upon the stage. . . . At last you make the discovery that you yourself look as queer as your neighbor.

Marion Randall, "Some Aspects of a Sierra Club Outing," *Sierra Club Bulletin* vol. 5, no. 3, January 1905

"Steve Wyckoff, Dot Leavitt, Ansel Adams in commissary at Crabtree Camp, July 28, 1932." "Young Tap," Helen LeConte, and legendary Sierra Club cook Don Tachet, famous for his pies, in background; Walter L. Huber, photographer; Dorothy Leavitt Pepper, *Photographs from a Trip to Yellowstone National Park*

Renowned photographer Ansel Adams was given his first camera while on a camping trip to Yosemite in 1916, when he was fourteen. He became a lifelong member of the Sierra Club at age seventeen, and while in the mountains in 1927 discovered that he could make photographs that were, as he said, "an austere and blazing poetry of the real."

Photograph taken in Marin County (?), California, circa 1905; Myrtle Rossiter Saunders, San Francisco Bay Area Scenes

1. **D**on't wear your pocket handkerchief tied to your belt, or your teaspoon tucked in your shoe— the police might regard you with suspicion.

2. Don't dig "hip holes" in the mattress.

3. Don't forget that teeth brushing and bathing, though done on a larger scale, must be confined to the bathroom for the next eleven months.

4. On your return to civilization, conversation will be mixed with food.

5. Don't bury your head in your plate until it's empty, then rush behind your host's chair and line up for seconds.

6. Don't cut your meat with your teaspoon.

7. When you arise from the table, don't brush off the seat of your trousers.

Olive Miller, "Dinner Don'ts for Returned Sierrans," circa 1916, manuscript, from the Irma Weill Papers

We are again on the plains of Sacramento, but we no longer find the heat oppressive. We have been all along the road mistaken for horse or cattle drovers, or for emigrants just across the plains. We were often greeted with "Where's your drove?" or "How long across the plains?" We have been in camp nearly six weeks, and ridden five or six hundred miles. Burned skin, dusty hair and clothes, flannel shirt, breeches torn, and coarse, heavy boots; the mistake is quite natural. Home to-day! Hurrah! We rode into Sacramento, 10 miles, in 1½ hours, galloping nearly the whole way. We went at a good gallop in the regular order — double file — through the streets of Sacramento, the whole length of the city, down to the wharf and there tied our horses. Everybody crowded around, especially the little boys about the wharf curious to know "who and what were these in strange attire."

... "Aren't you the party who went galloping down the street just now?"

"Yes."

"Where are you from?"

"Only a pleasure party."

"Why, I thought you were outlaws, or cattle-drovers, or horse-dealers, or emigrants over the plains, or something of that kind."

Joseph LeConte, *A Journal of Ramblings through the High Sierras of California by the "University Excursion Party"* (San Francisco: Francis & Valentine, 1875)

Muir Club, Girls' Outing, San Joaquin River and Evolution Basin, 1924, Leonarde Keeler Photograph Collection

Once the tent stakes had been pulled up and the duffle bags stuffed with sooty pots and mountain duds redolent of many campfires, returning campers yearned for the luxuries of home—for ice cream, hamburgers, mail, music, and watermelon.

The Bancroft Library

The Bancroft Library is the primary special collections library at the University of California, Berkeley. One of the largest and most heavily used libraries of manuscripts, rare books, and unique materials in the United States, Bancroft supports major research and instructional activities. The library's largest resource is the Bancroft Collection of Western Americana, which was begun by Hubert Howe Bancroft in the 1860s and which documents through primary and secondary resources in a variety of formats the social, political, economic, and cultural history of the region from the western plains states to the Pacific coast and from Panama to Alaska, with greatest emphasis on California and Mexico from the late eighteenth century to the present. The Bancroft Library is also home to the Rare Book and Literary Manuscript Collections, the Regional Oral History Office, the History of Science and Technology Collections, the Mark Twain Papers and Project, the University Archives, the Pictorial Collections, and the Center for the Tebtunis Papyri. For more information, see the library's website at http://bancroft.berkeley.edu.

For information on the Friends of The Bancroft Library, to make a gift or donation, or if you have other questions please contact:

Friends of The Bancroft Library
University of California, Berkeley
Berkeley, Calfornia 94720-6000
(510) 642-3782

Heyday
HEYDAY INSTITUTE

Since its founding in 1974, Heyday Books has occupied a unique niche in the publishing world, specializing in books that foster an understanding of California history, literature, art, environment, social issues, and culture. We are a 501(c)(3) nonprofit organization committed to providing a platform for writers, poets, artists, scholars, and storytellers who help keep California's diverse legacy alive.

We are grateful for the generous funding we've received for our publications and programs during the past year from various foundations and more than three hundred individuals. Major recent supporters include: Anonymous; Anthony Andreas, Jr.; Arroyo Fund; Barnes & Noble bookstores; Bay Tree Fund; California Association of Resource Conservation Districts; California Oak Foundation; Candelaria Fund; CANfit; Columbia Foundation; Colusa Indian Community Council; Wallace Alexander Gerbode Foundation; Richard & Rhoda Goldman Fund; Evelyn & Walter Haas, Jr. Fund; Walter & Elise Haas Fund; Hopland Band of Pomo Indians; James Irvine Foundation; Guy Lampard & Suzanne Badenhoop; Jeff Lustig; George Frederick Jewett Foundation; LEF Foundation; David Mas Masumoto; James McClatchy; Michael McCone; Gordon & Betty Moore Foundation; Morongo Band of Mission Indians; National Endowment for the Arts; National Park Service; Ed Penhoet; Poets & Writers; Rim of the World Interpretive Association; Riverside/San Bernardino County Indian Health; River Rock Casino; Alan Rosenus; John-Austin Saviano/ Moore Foundation; Sandy Cold Shapero; Ernest & June Siva; L.J. Skaggs and Mary C. Skaggs Foundation; Swinerton Family Fund; Susan Swig Watkins; and the Harold & Alma White Memorial Fund.

Heyday Institute Board of Directors
Michael McCone, chair
Bob Callahan
Peter Dunckel
Karyn Flynn
Theresa Harlan
Jack Hicks
Leanne Hinton
Nancy Hom
Susan Ives
Guy Lampard
Linda Norton
Lee Swenson
Jim Swinerton
Lynne Withey
Stan Yogi

For more information about Heyday Institute, our publications and programs, please visit our website at www.heydaybooks.com.

PHOTOGRAPH BY RICHARD NEIDHARDT

SUSAN SNYDER worked as a teacher, illustrator, and Japanese language interpreter before landing in The Bancroft Library at the University of California, Berkeley, where she has spent ten years as a lucky denizen of its stacks, foxholes, attics, and moats. She is the author of *Bear in Mind: The California Grizzly*, also available from Heyday Books.